BIG DATA ANALYTICS
Made Easy

BIG DATA
ANALYTICS
Made Easy

Y. LAKSHMI PRASAD

Notion Press

Old No. 38, New No. 6
McNichols Road, Chetpet
Chennai - 600 031

First Published by Notion Press 2016
Copyright © Y. Lakshmi Prasad 2016
All Rights Reserved.

ISBN 978-1-946390-71-4

This book is dedicated to

A.P.J. Abdul Kalam

(Thinking should become your capital asset, no matter whatever ups and downs you come across in your life.)

To download the data files used in this book, please use the below link:

www.praanalytix.com/Bigdata-Analytics-MadeEasy-Datafiles.rar

Contents

Preface

This book is an indispensable guide focuses on Machine Learning and R Programming, in an instructive and conversational tone which helps them who want to make their career in Big Data Analytics/ Data Science and entry level Data Scientist for their day to day tasks with practical examples, detailed description, Issues, Resolutions, key techniques and many more.

This book is like your personal trainer, explains the art of Big data Analytics/ Data Science with R Programming in 18 steps which covers from Statistics, Unsupervised Learning, Supervised Learning as well as Ensemble Learning. Many Machine Learning Concepts are explained in an easy way so that you feel confident while using them in Programming. If you are already working as a Data Analyst, still you need this book to sharpen your skills. This book will be an asset to you and your career by making you a better Data Scientist.

Author's Note

One interesting thing in Big Data Analytics, it is the career Option for people with various study backgrounds. I have seen Data Analyst/Business Analyst/Data Scientists with different qualifications like M.B.A, Statistics, M.C.A, M. Tech, M.sc Mathematics and many more. It is wonderful to see people with different backgrounds working on the same project, but how can we expect Machine Learning and Domain knowledge from a person with technical qualification.

Every person might be strong in their own subject but Data Scientist needs to know more than one subject (Programming, Machine Learning, Mathematics, Business Acumen and Statistics). This might be the reason I thought it would be beneficial to have a resource that brings together all these aspects in one volume so that it would help everybody who wants to make Big Data Analytics/ Data Science as their career Option.

This book was written to assist learners in getting started, while at the same time providing techniques that I have found to be useful to Entry level Data Analyst and R programmers. This book is aimed more at the R programmer who is responsible for providing insights on both structured and unstructured data.

This book assumes that the reader has no prior knowledge of Machine Learning and R programming. Each one of us has our own style of approach to an issue; it is likely that others will find alternate solutions for many of the issues discussed in this book. The sample data that appears in a number of examples throughout this book was just an imaginary, any resemblance was simply accidental.

This book was organized in 18 Steps from introduction to Ensemble Learning, which offers the different thinking patterns in Data Scientist work environment. The solutions to some of the questions are not written fully but only some steps of hints are mentioned. It is just for the sake of recalling the memory involving important facts in common practice.

Y. Lakshmi Prasad

Acknoweldgements

A great deal of information was received from the numerous people who offered their time. I would like to thank each and every person who helped me in creating this book.

I heartily express my gratitude to all of my peers, ISB colleagues, friends and students whose sincere response geared up to meet the exigent way of expressing the contents. I am very much grateful to our Press, editors and designers whose scrupulous assistance completed this work to reach your hands.

Finally, I am personally indebted to my wonderful partner *Prajwala*, and my kid *Prakhyath*, for their support, enthusiasm, and tolerance without which this book would have never been completed.

Y. Lakshmi Prasad

STEP 1

Introduction to Big Data Analytics

1.1 WHAT BIG DATA?

Big Data is any voluminous amount of **Structured, Semi-structured** and **Unstructured** data that has the potential to be mined for information where the Individual records stop mattering and only aggregates matter. Data becomes Big data when it is difficult to process using traditional techniques.

1.2 CHARACTERISTICS OF BIG DATA:

There are many characteristics of Big data. Let me discuss a few here.

1. **Volume:** Big data implies enormous volumes of data generated by Sensors, Machines combined with internet explosion, social media, e-commerce, GPS devices etc.

2. **Velocity:** It implies to the rate at which the data is pouring in like Facebook users generate 3 million likes per day and around 450 million of tweets are created per day by users.

3. **Variety:** It implies to the type of formats and they can be classified into 3 types:
   - Structured – RDBMS like Oracle, MySQL, Legacy systems like Excel, Access
   - Semi- Structured – Emails, Tweets, Log files, User reviews
   - Un-Structured – Photos, Video, Audio files.

4. **Veracity:** It refers to the biases, noise, and abnormality in data. If we want meaningful insight from this data we need to cleanse it initially.

5. **Validity:** It refers to appropriateness and precision of the data since the validity of the data is very important to make decisions.

6. **Volatility:** It refers to how long the data is valid since the data which is valid right now might not be valid just a few minutes or fewer days later.

1.3 WHY BIG DATA IMPORTANT?

The success of the organization not just lies in how good there are in doing their business but also on how well they can analyze their data and derive insights about their company, their competitors etc. Big data can help you in taking the right decision at right time.

Why not RDBMS? Scalability is the major problem in RDBMS, it is very difficult to manage RDBMS when the requirements or the number of users change. One more problem with RDBMS is that we need to decide the structure of the database at the start and making any changes later might be a huge task. While dealing with Big data we need flexibility and unfortunately, RDBMS cannot provide that.

1.4 ANALYTICS TERMINOLOGY

Analytics is one of the few fields where a lot of different terms thrown around by everyone and lot of these terms sound similar to each other yet they are used in different contexts. There are some terms which sound very different to each other yet they are similar and can be used interchangeably. Someone who is new to Analytics expected to confuse with this abundance of terminology which is there in this field.

Analytics is the process of breaking the problem into simpler parts and using inferences based on data to take decisions. Analytics is not a tool or technology, rather it is a way of thinking and acting. Business Analytics specifies application of Analytics in the sphere of Business. It includes Marketing Analytics, Risk Analytics, Fraud Analytics, CRM Analytics, Loyalty Analytics, Operation Analytics as well as HR analytics. Within the business, Analytics is used in all sorts of industries like Finance Analytics, Healthcare Analytics, Retail analytics, Telecom Analytics, Web Analytics. Predictive Analytics is gained popularity in the recent past Vs. Retrospective nature such as OLAP and BI, Descriptive analytics is to describe or explore any kind of data. Data exploration and Data Preparation is essential to rely heavily on descriptive analytics. **Big Data Analytics** is the new term which is used to Analyze the unstructured data and big data like terabytes or even petabytes of data. Big Data is any data set which cannot be analyzed with conventional tools.

1.5 TYPES OF ANALYTICS

Analytics can be applied to so many problems and in so many different industries that it becomes important to take some time to understand the scope of analytics in business.

Classifying the different type of analytics. We are going to look closer at 3 broad classifications of analytics: 1. Based on the Industry. 2. Based on the Business function 3. Based of kind of insights offered.

Let's start by looking at industries where analytics usage is very prevalent. There are certain industries which have always created a huge amount of data like Credit cards and consumer goods. These industries were among the first ones to adopt analytics. Analytics is often classified on the basis of the industry it is being applied to, hence you will hear terms such as insurance analytics, retail analytics, web analytics and so on. We can even classify analytics on the basis of the business function it's used in. Classification of analytics on the basis of business function and impact goes as follows:

- Marketing Analytics
- Sales and HR analytics
- Supply chain analytics and so on

This can be a equitably long list as analytics has the prospective to impact virtually any business activity within a large organization. But the most popular way of classifying analytics is on the basis of what it allows us to do. All the information is collected different industries and different departments. All we need to do is slicing and dicing the data in diverse ways, maybe looking at it from different angles or along different dimensions etc.

As you can see descriptive analysis is possibly the simplest type of analytics to perform simply because it uses existing information from the past, to understand decisions in the present and hopefully helps decide an effective source of action in the future. However, because of its relative ease of understanding and application descriptive analytics has been often considered the subdued twin of analytics. But it is also extremely powerful in its potential and in most business situations, Descriptive analytics can help address most problems.

Retailers are very interested in understanding the relationship between products. They want to know if the person buys a product A, is he also likely buying product B or product C. This is called product affinity analysis or association analysis and it is commonly used in the retail industry. It is also called market basket analysis and is used to refer a set of techniques that can be applied to analyze the shopping basket or a transaction. Have you ever wondered why milk is placed right at the back of the store while magazines and chewing gum are right by the check-out? That is because through analytics retailers realize that while traveling all the way to the back of the store to pick up your essentials, you just may be tempted to pick up something else and also because magazines and chewing gum are cheap impulse buys. You decide to throw them in your cart since they are not too expensive and you have probably been eying them as you waited in line at the counter.

Predictive Analytics works by identifying patterns and historical data and then using statistics to make inferences about the future. At a very simplistic level, we try to fit the data into a certain pattern and if we believe the data is following a certain pattern then we can predict what will happen in the future. Let's try and look at another example involving predictive analytics in the telecom industry. A large telecom company has access to all kinds of information about its customer's calling habits:

- How much time do they spend on the phone, How many international calls do they make?
- Do they prefer SMS or call numbers outside their city?

This is information one can obtain purely by observation or descriptive analytics. But such companies would, more importantly, like to know which is the customers plan to leave and take a new connection with their competitors. This will use historical information but rely on predictive modeling and analysis to obtain results. This is predictive analysis. While descriptive analytics is a very powerful tool. It stills gives us information only about the past whereas, in reality, most user's primary concern will always be the future. A hotel owner would want to predict how many of his rooms will be occupied next week. The CEO of the Pharma Company will want to know which of his under test drugs is most likely to succeed. This is where predictive analytics is a lot more useful. In addition to these tools, there is a third type of analytics, which came into existence very recently, maybe just a decade old. This is called prescriptive analytics. Prescriptive analytics goes beyond predictive analytics by not only telling you what is going on but also what might happen and most importantly what to do about it. It could also inform you about the impact of these decisions, which is what makes prescriptive analytics so cutting edge. Business domains that are great examples were prescriptive analytics can be used are the aviation industry or nationwide road networks. Prescriptive analytics can predict an effectively correct road bottlenecks, or identify roads where tolls can be implemented to streamline traffic. To see how prescriptive analytics functions in the aviation industry, let's look at the following example.

Airlines are always looking for ways to optimize their routes for maximum efficiency. This can be billions of dollars in savings but this is not that easy to do. With over 50 million commercial flights in the world every year, that's a flight every second. Just a simple flight route between two cities, let's say, San Francisco and Boston, has a possibility of 2000 route options. So the aviation industry often relies on prescriptive analytics to decide what, which and how they should fly their airplanes to keep cost down and profits up. So, we have taken a fairly in-depth look at descriptive, predictive and prescriptive analytics. The focus of this course is going to be descriptive analytics. Towards the end, we will also spend some time on understanding some of the more popular predictive modeling techniques.

1.6 ANALYTICS LIFECYCLE

The Analytics lifecycle has different stages and many people describe it in many ways, but the overall idea remains same. here let us consider the following stages of an Analytics project lifecycle.

- Problem Identification
- Hypothesis Formulation
- Data Collection

- Data Exploration
- Data Preparation/ Manipulation
- Model planning / Building
- Validate Model
- Evaluate/Monitor results

1. **Problem Identification:** A problem is a situation that is judged as something that needs to be corrected. It is our job to make sure we are solving the right problem, it may not be the one presented to us by the client. What do we really need to solve?

   Sometimes the problem statements that we get from the business are very straight forward. For example:

   - How do I identify the most valuable customers?
   - How do I ensure that I minimize losses from the product not being available on the shelf?
   - How do I optimize my inventory?
   - How do I detect customers that are likely to default on a bill payment?

These are straight forward problem statements and there is really no confusion around what is it that we are trying to achieve with an analytical project. However, every single time our business statement may not lead to clear problem identification. Sometimes, the business statements are very high level and therefore you will need to spend time with the business to understand the needs and obtain the context. You may need to break down that issue into sub-issues to identify critical requirements. You may need to think about the constraints that need to be included in the solution.

Let us take an example for this. Supposing that you work for a credit card company, and the business tell you that this is the problem statement that they want you to look at, which is "We want to receive credit care applications only from good customers" Now from a business perspective, is this a valid business statement? Certainly, at a very high level, this is a valid business requirement. However, for your purpose which is to build a solution to address this question, is this a very valid statement or is it a sufficient starting point for the data analysis? No. Because, there are multiple problems with a business statement like this, which is, we want to receive credit care applications only from good customers. Let us look at the problem with that problem statement. I want to receive credit care applications only from good customers. One of the most obvious problem with that statement is who are good customers?

If you have any knowledge of the credit card industry, one of the answers for a good customer could be people that don't default on payments. That is, you spend on the credit card and you pay the credit card company back on time. However, another definition of a good customer could be people who don't pay on time. Why is that? Because, if you don't pay on time, the credit card company has the opportunity to charge you high rates of interest on that balance on your credit card. These kinds of customers are called revolvers. Who really is the good customer for a credit card company? Are these customers who pay on time? Or are these customers that default and don't pay on time. An answer could be both are good customers. How is that possible? It really depends on your perspective.

If you are interested in minimizing risk, if you work in the risk function of the credit card company, your definition of a good customer is the customers that pay on time, customers that don't default. Whereas, if you were looking at revenue, then your perspective on a good customer could be people who spend a lot on the credit card and don't pay it all back. They have a high revolving balance. Now, as an analyst, who decides who good customers are? When the credit card company gives you a business statement that says we want to accept credit card application from only good customers. Do you know that they are looking at risk or revenue? It really depends on the business interest; it depends on the business goals for that year. In fact, a good customer this year may be a bad customer next year. This is why it is important to obtain the context or the problem statement before starting on an analysis. But this is not the only problem with this problem statement.

Another problem is thinking about the decision which is, can you really insist on receiving good applications or can you insist on approving good applications. Is the decision at the application stage or the approval stage? Can you really control applications to be good or can you control the decisions to enable only good customers to come on to you?. Another problem with this problem statement is that we only want to receive credit card applications from good customers. Is it realistic for you to assume that you will have a solution that will never accept a bad customer? Again, not a realistic outcome. Coming back to our problem definition state which is, given a business problem, I want to get good customers as a credit card company. How do you frame that problem into something that analytical approach can tackle?

One way is to add specifics to the problem statement. So, think about specific, measurable, attainable, realistic, and timely outcomes that you can attach to that problem statement. That is, why we emphasize that you need to understand the business context thoroughly and talk to the business that you are tackling the right problem. How would I be able to add specifics to this problem statement? Let us assume that I am looking at it from the risk perspective, because in this year my credit card companies focused on reducing the portfolio risk. So, I could have a variety of business problem statements. For example, reduce losses from credit card default by at least 30 percent in the first 12 months post implementation of the new strategy.

Develop an algorithm to screen applications that do not meet good customer defined criteria that will reduce defaults by 20 percent in the next 3 months. Identify strategies to reduce defaults by 20 percent in the next three months by allowing at-risk customers additional payment options. We have decided that the good problem definition is something that we are tackling from a risk perspective. But, for the same business statement, we now have three different problem statements that are tackling three different things. Again, which of these should I choose as a starting point for my analysis? Should I identify strategies for my existing customers or should I look at identifying potential new customers? Again, this is something that may be driven by business needs. So, it is important to constantly talk to the business to make sure that when you are starting an analytics project you are tackling the right problem statement.

Getting to a clearly defined problem is often discovery driven – Start with a conceptual definition and through analysis (root cause, impact analysis, etc.) you shape and redefine the problem in terms of issues. A problem becomes known when a person observes a discrepancy between the way things are and the way things ought to be. Problems can be identified through:

- Comparative/benchmarking studies
- Performance reporting - assessment of current performance against goals and objectives
- SWOT Analysis – assessment of strengths, weaknesses, opportunities, and threats
- Complaints/ Surveys

Sometimes the thing we think is a problem is not the real problem, so to get at the real problem, probing is necessary. Root Cause Analysis is an effective method of probing – it helps identify what, how, and why something happened.

Let us consider an employee turnover rate in our organization is increasing. we need to find out Five Why's refers to the practice of asking, five times, why the problem exists in order to get to the root cause of the problem:

- Why are Employees leaving for other jobs?
- Why are Employees not satisfied?
- Why do Employees feel that they are underpaid?
- Why are Other employers paying higher salaries?
- Why Demand for such employees has increased in the market?

Basic Questions to Ask in Defining the Problem:

- Who is causing the problem?
- Who are impacted by this problem?
- What will happen if this problem is not solved? What are the impacts?
- Where and When does this problem occur?
- Why is this problem occurring?
- How should the process work?
- How are people currently handling the problem?

2.   **Formulating the hypothesis:** Break down problems and formulate hypotheses. Frame the Questions which need to be answered or topics which need to be explored in order to solve a problem.

   ◆   Develop a comprehensive list of all possible issues related to the problem

   ◆   Reduce the comprehensive list by eliminating duplicates and combining overlapping issues

   ◆   Using consensus building, get down to a major issues list.

3.   **Data Collection:** In order to answer the key questions and validate the hypotheses collection of realistic information is necessary. Depending on the type of problem being solved, different data collection techniques may be used. Data collection is a critical stage in problem solving - if it is superficial, biased or incomplete, data analysis will be difficult.

   ### Data Collection Techniques:

   ◆   Using data that has already been collected by others

   ◆   Systematically selecting and watching characteristics of people, objects or events.

   ◆   Oral questioning of respondents, either individually or as a group.

   ◆   Collecting data based on answers provided by respondents in written form.

   ◆   Facilitating free discussions on specific topics with selected group of participants.

4.   **Data Exploration:** Before a formal data analysis can be conducted, the analyst must know how many cases are in the dataset, what variables are included, how many missing observations there are and what general hypotheses the data is likely to support. An initial exploration of the dataset helps answer these questions by familiarizing analysts about the data with which they are working.

   Analysts commonly use visualization for data exploration because it allows users to quickly and simply view most of the relevant features of their dataset. By doing this, users can identify variables that are likely to have interesting observations. By displaying data graphically through scatter plots or bar charts users can see if two or more variables correlate and determine if they are good candidates for further in-depth analysis.

5.   **Data Preparation:** Data comes to you in a form that is not easy to analyze. We need to clean data and check it for consistency, extensive manipulation of the data is needed in order to analyze.

   Data Preparation steps may include:

   ▪   Importing the data
   ▪   Variable Identification/ Creating New variables
   ▪   Checking and summarizing the data
   ▪   Selecting subsets of the data

- Selecting and managing variables.
- Combining data
- Splitting data into many datasets.
- Missing values treatment
- Outlier treatment

Variable Identification: First, identify Predictor (Input) and Target (output) variables. Then, identify the data type and category of the variables.

Univariate Analysis: At this stage, we explore variables one by one. Method to perform Univariate analysis will depend on whether the variable type is categorical or continuous. Let's look at these methods and statistical measures for categorical and continuous variables individually.

Continuous Variables: In the case of continuous variables, we need to understand the central tendency and spread of the variable. These are measured using diverse statistical metrics visualization methods.

Categorical Variables: For categorical variables, we use a frequency table to understand the distribution of each category. We can also read as a percentage of values under each category. It can be measured using two metrics, Count and Percent against each category.

6. **Model Building**: This is really the entire process of building the solution and implementing the solution. The majority of the project time spent in the solution implementation stage. One interesting thing to remember with an analytical approach is that an analytical approach when you are building models, analytical models, is a very iterative process because there is no such thing as a final solution or a perfect solution. Typically, you will spend time building multiple models on multiple solutions before arriving at the best solution that the business will work with.

7. There are many ways of taking decisions from a business perspective. Analytics is one way. There are others ways of taking a decision. It could be experience based decision taking. It could be gut-based decision making. And not every single time you will always choose an analytical approach. However, in the long run, it makes sense to build analytical capability because that leads to more objective decision making. But fundamentally if you want to data to drive decision making, you need to make sure that you have invested in collecting the right data to enable your decision-making through data.

8. **Model Evaluation/Monitoring**: This is an ongoing process essentially aimed at looking at the effectiveness of the solution over time. Remember that an analytical problem-solving approach, which is different from the standard problem-solving approach. We need to remember these points:

   - There is a clear confidence on data to drive solution identification.
   - We are using analytical techniques based on numeric theories.

- ◆ You need to have a good understanding of theoretical concepts to business situations in order to build a feasible solution.

What that means is you need to a good understanding of the business situation and the business context and as well a strong knowledge of analytical approaches and be able to merge the concepts, come up with a workable solution. In some industries, the rate of change is very high. So, solutions age very fast. In other industries, the rate of change may not be as high and when you build a solution, you may have 2-3 years where your solution works well but post that will need to be tweaked to manage the new business conditions. But, the way to assess whether or not your solution is working, is to periodically check solution effectiveness.

You need to track dependability over time and you may need to make minor changes to bring the solution back on track. Sometimes, may have to build an entire solution from scratch because the environment has changed so dramatically that the solution that you built does not clutch anymore in the current business context.

1.7 COMMON MISTAKES IN ANALYTICAL THINKING

The client's definition of the problem may not be correct. He may lack the knowledge and experience that you have. Since most problems are not unique, We may be able to corroborate the problem and possible solutions against other sources. The best solutions to a problem are often too difficult for the client to implement. So be cautious about recommending the optimal solution to a problem. Most explanations require some degree of conciliation for execution.

STEP 2

Getting started with R

2.1 INTRODUCTION

R is a programming language for statistical analysis and reporting. R is a simple programming language which includes many functions for Data Analytics, it has an effective data handling and storage facility. R provides graphical facilities for data analysis and reporting. I request you to please Install R and R studio which is freely downloadable. Here in my book I use the code written in R studio. To work in R studio, you need to have even R at the back end, so please go to site CRAN and Install latest version of R according to your Operating system. So Let's Start (Rock and Roll) with R-Studio:

When you first open the R-studio, you will see four windows.

1. **Scripts:** Serves as an area to write and save R code
2. **Workspace:** Lists the datasets and variables in the R environment
3. **Plots:** Displays the plots generated by the R code
4. **Console** Provides a history of the executed R code and the output.

2.2 ELEMENTARY OPERATIONS IN R

1. Expressions:

if you are working with only numbers R can be used as an advanced calculator, just type

    4+5

and press enter, you will get the value 9.

R can perform mathematical calculations without obligation that you need to store it in an object.

The result is printed on the console.

Try calculating the product of 2 or more numbers (* is the multiplication operator).

    6*9 # you will get 54.

✓   **Anything written after # sign will be considered as comments in R.**

✓   R follows BODMAS rules to perform mathematical operations.

Type the following commands and understand the difference.

20–15*2 # you will get -10

(20–15)*2 #here you will get 10

Be careful of dividing any value with 0 will give you **inf** (infinity).

type this command in the console and check

8/0

These mathematical operations can be combined into long formulae to achieve specific tasks.

2. Logical Values:

Few expressions return a "logical value": TRUE or FALSE. (known as "Boolean" values.)

Look at the expression that gives us a logical value:

6<9 #TRUE

3. Variables:

We can store values into a variable to access it later.

X <- 48 #to store a value in x.

Y <- "YL, Prasad" (Don't forget the quotes)

Now X and Y are the objects created in R, can be used in expressions in the position of the original result.

Try to call X and Y just by typing the object name

Y # [1] "YL, Prasad"

we need to remember that R is case sensitive. if you assign a value to cap X and call small x then it will show you an error.

Try dividing X by 2 (/ is the division operator) # you will get 24 as the answer

We can re-assign any value to a variable at any time. Assign "Lakshmi" to Y.

Y <- "Lakshmi"

We can print the value of a variable just by typing its name in the console. Try printing the current value of Y.

If you wrote this code, congratulations! You wrote the first code in R and created an object.

4. Functions:

We can call a function by typing its name, followed by arguments to that function in parenthesis.

Try the sum function, to add up a few numbers. Enter:

sum(1, 3, 5) #9

We use sqrt function to get the square root of 16.

sqrt(16) #4

16^.5 #also gives the same answer as 4

Square root transformation is the most widely used transformation along with log transformation in data preparation.

Type the following commands and check the answers

log(1) #0

log(10) #2.302585

log10(100) # this will return 2 since the log of 100 to the base 10 is 2.

anytime if you want to access the help window you can type the following commands

help(exp)

?exp

If you want some example for functions you give this command:

example(log)

R allows one to save the workspace environment, including variables and loaded libraries, into a **.R** data file using the save.image() function. An existing .R data file can be loaded using the load.image() function.

5. Files

R commands can be written and stored in plain text files (with ".R" extension) for executing later.

Assume that we stored some sample scripts, We can list the files in the current directory from within R, by calling the list.files function.

list.files()

2.3 SETTING UP A WORKING DIRECTORY

Before getting deeper into R it is always better to set up a working directory to store all our files, scalars, vectors, data frames etc. For this first, we want to know what is the current directory R is using by default. to understand that, type the command:

getwd() # [1] "C:/Users/admin/Documents"

Now I want to set folder R data as my working directory which is located in D drive. to do this I will give the command:

setwd("D:/R data")

Press enter (Click Submit Icon) to make sure that your command has been executed and the working directory been set. We set the folder R data in D drive as working directory. It doesn't mean that we created anything new here, but just assigned a place as the working directory, this is where all the files will be added.

to check whether the working directory has set up correctly give the command:

getwd()

2.4 DATA STRUCTURES IN R

A data structure is an interface to data organized in computer memory. R provides several kinds of data structure each designed to optimize some aspect of storage, access, or processing.

Examples of Data structures:1.Vector 2.Matrix 3.Factor 4.Data Frame

1. Vectors

Vectors are a basic building block for data in R. R variables are actually vectors. A vector can only consist of values in the same class. The tests for vectors can be conducted using the is.vector() function.

The name may sound frightening, but a vector is simply a list of values. A vector's values can be numbers, strings, logical values, or any other type, as long as they are all the same type.

Types of Vectors: Integer, Numeric, Logical, Character, Complex.

R provides functionality that enables the easy creation and manipulation of vectors. The following R code illustrates how a vector can be created using the combine function, c()

or the colon operator, :,

Let us create a vector of numbers:

c(4,7,9)

The c function (c is short for Combine) creates a new vector by combining a list of values.

Create a vector with strings:

c('a','b','c')

Sequence Vectors

We can create a vector with start:end notation to make sequences. Let us build a vector from the sequence of integers from 5 to 9.

5:9 # Creates a vector with values from 5 through 9:

We can even call the seq function. Let's try to do the same thing with seq:

seq(5,9)

Vector Access

After creating a vector with some strings in it and store it, We can retrieve an individual value within a vector by just providing its numeric index in square brackets.

sentence <- c('Learn', 'Data', 'Analytics')

sentence[3] # [1] "Analytics"

We can assign new values within an existing vector. Try changing the third word to "Science":

sentence [3] <- "Science"

If you add new values to the vector, the vector will grow to accommodate them. Let's add a fourth word:

sentence [4] <- 'By YL, Prasad'

We can use a vector within the square brackets to access multiple values.

Try getting the first and fourth words:

sentence [c(1, 4)]

This means you can retrieve ranges of values. Get the second through fourth words:

sentence [2:4]

We can set ranges of values, by just providing the values in a vector.

sentence [5:7] <- c('at', 'PRA', 'Analytix') # to add words 5 through 7

Try accessing the seventh word of the sentence vector:

sentence[7]

Vector Names

Let us create a 3-item vector, and store it in the ranks variable. We can assign names to a vector's elements by passing a second vector filled with names to the names assignment function, like this:

ranks <- 1:3

names(ranks) <- c("first", "second", "third")

ranks

We can use the names to access the vector's values.

ranks["first"]

2. Matrices

A matrix in R is a collection of homogeneous elements arranged in 2 dimensions.

- ◆ A matrix is a vector with a dim attribute, i.e. an integer vector giving the number or rows and columns
- ◆ The functions dim(), nrow() and ncol provide the attributes of the matrix.
- ◆ Rows and columns can have names, dimnames(), rownames(), colnames()

Let us look at the basics of working with matrices, creating them, accessing them and plotting them.

Let us create a matrix 3 rows high by 4 columns wide, with all its fields set to 0.

Sample <- matrix (0, 3, 4)

Matrix Construction

We can construct a matrix directly with data elements, the matrix content is filled along the column orientation by default.

Look at the following code, the content of Sample is filled with the columns consecutively.

Sample <- matrix(1:20, nrow=4, ncol=5)

Matrix Access

To obtain values from matrices you just have to provide two indices instead of one.

Let's print our Sample matrix:

print (Sample)

Try getting the value from the second row in the third column of Sample:

Sample [2,3]

We can get an entire row of the matrix by omitting the column index (but keep the comma). Try retrieving the Third row:

Sample [3,] # [1] 3 7 11 15

To get an entire column, omit the row index. Retrieve the fourth column:

Sample [,4] # [1] 13 14 15 16

3. Factors

When we want the data to be grouped by category, R has a special type called a factor to track these categorized values. A factor is a vector whose elements can take on one of a specific set of values. For example, "Gender" will usually take on only the values "Male", "Female" and "NA". The set of values that the elements of a factor can take is called its levels.

Creating Factors

To categorize the values, simply pass the vector to the factor function:

> *gender <- c('male', 'female', 'male', 'NA', 'female')*
>
> *types <- factor(gender)*
>
> *print(gender)*

You see the raw list of strings, repeated values and all. Now print the types factor:

> *print(types)*

Let's take a look at the underlying integers. Pass the factor to the as.integer function:

> *as.integer(types) # [1] 2 1 2 3 1*

You can get only the factor levels with the levels function:

> *levels(types) # [1] "female" "male" "NA"*

4. Data Frames

data frames provide a structure for storing and accessing several variables of possibly different data types. Because of their flexibility to handle many data types, data frames are the preferred input format for many of the modeling functions available in R.

Let us create three individual objects named Id, Gender, and Age and tie them together into a data set.

> *Id <- c(101, 102, 103, 104, 105)*
>
> *Gender <- c('male', 'female', 'male', 'NA', 'female')*
>
> *Age <- c(38,29,NA,46,53)*

The Id, Gender, and Age are three individual objects, R has a structure known as the data frame which can tie all these variables together in a single table or an Excel spreadsheet. It has a specific number of columns, each of which is expected to contain values of a particular type. It also has an indeterminate number of rows - sets of related values for each column.

It's easy to create a dataset just call the data.frame function, and pass Id, Gender, and Age as the arguments. Assign the result to the Test dataset:

> *Test <- data.frame(Id, Gender, Age)*

Print Test to see its contents:

> *print(Test)*
>
> *fix(Test) #To view this object data set*

Data Frame Access: It is easy to access individual portions of a data frame. We can get individual columns by providing their index number in double-brackets. Try getting the second column (Gender) of Test:

Test[[2]]

You could provide a column name as a string in double-brackets for more readability

Test[["Age"]]

We can even use a shorthand notation: the data frame name, a dollar sign, and the column name without quotes.

Test$Gender

2.5 IMPORTING AND EXPORTING DATA

Quite often we need to get our data from external files like Text files, excel sheets and CSV files, to perform this R was given the capability to easily load data in from external files.

Your environment might have many objects and values, which you can delete using the following code:

rm(list=ls())

The rm() function allows you to remove objects from a specified environment.

Importing TXT files: If you have a .txt or a tab-delimited text file, you can easily import it with the basic R function read.table().

setwd("D:/R data")

Inc_ds <- read.table("Income.txt")

For files that use separator strings other than commas, you can use the read.table function. The **sep=** argument defines the separator character, and you can specify a tab character with "\t". Call read.table on "Inc_tab.txt", using tab separators:

read.table("Inc_tab.txt ", sep="\t")

Notice the "V1","V2" and "V3" column headers? The first line is not automatically treated as column headers with read.table. This behavior is controlled by the header argument. Call read.table again, setting header to TRUE:

Inc_th <- read.table("Inc_tab.txt", sep="\t", header=TRUE)

fix(Inc_th)

Importing CSV Files: If you have a file that separates the values with a comma you usually are dealing with a .csv file. You can load a CSV file's content into a data frame by passing the file name to the read.CSV function.

read.CSV("Employee.csv") #To perform this R expects presence of our files in working directory.

2.5 Exporting files using the write.table function: The write.table function outputs data files. The first argument specifies which data frame in R is to be exported. The next argument specifies the file to be created. The default separator is a blank space but any separator can be specified in the **sep=** option. Since we do not wish to include row names we were given option row.names=FALSE, The default setting for the quote option is to include quotes around all the character values, i.e., around values in string variables and around the column names. As we have shown in the example it is very common not to want the quotes when creating a text file.

write.table(Employee, file="emp.txt", row.names = FALSE, quote = FALSE)

STEP 3

Data Exploration

3.1 INTRODUCTION

Whenever we are about to create a model it is very important to understand the data and find the hidden insights of the data. the success of a data analysis project requires a deep understanding of the data. Data exploration will help you to create accurate models if you perform this in a planned way. Before a formal data analysis can be conducted, the analyst must know how many cases are in the dataset, what variables are included, how many missing observations there are in the dataset. Data exploration Steps includes Understanding the datasets and variables, Checking attributes of the data, Recognize and treat missing values, outliers, Understanding basic presentation of the data etc. Data exploration activities include the study of the data in terms of basic statistical measures and creation of graphs and plots to visualize and identify relationships and patterns.

An initial exploration of the dataset helps answer these questions by familiarizing analysts about the data with which they are working. Additional questions and considerations for the data conditioning step includes, What are the data sources? What are the target fields? How clean the data is? How consistent are the contents and files? Being a Data Scientist, you need to determine to what degree the data contains missing or inconsistent values and if the data contains values deviating from normal and Assess the consistency of the data types. For instance, if the team expects certain data to be numeric, confirm it is numeric or if it is a mixture of alphanumeric strings and text. Review the content of data columns or other inputs, and check to ensure they make sense. For instance, if the project involves analyzing income levels, preview the data to confirm that the income values are positive or if it is acceptable to have zeros or negative values.

Look for any evidence of systematic error. Examples include data feeds from sensors or other data sources breaking without anyone noticing, which causes invalid, incorrect, or missing data values. Review the data to gauge if the definition of the data is the same for all measurements. In some cases, a data column is repurposed, or the column stops being populated, without this change being annotated or without others being notified. After the team has collected and obtained at least some of the datasets needed for the subsequent analysis, a useful step is to leverage data visualization tools to look at high-level patterns in the data enables one to understand characteristics about the data very quickly. One example is using data visualization to examine data quality, such as whether the data contains many unexpected values or other indicators of dirty data. Another example is Skewness, such as if the majority of the data is heavily shifted toward one value or end of a continuum.

Data Visualization enables the user to find areas of interest, zoom, and filter to find more detailed information about a particular area of the data, and then find the detailed data behind a particular area. This approach provides a high-level view of the data and a great deal of information about a given dataset in a relatively short period of time.

3.2 GUIDELINES AND CONSIDERATIONS

Review data to ensure that calculations remained consistent within columns or across tables for a given data field. For instance, did customer lifetime value change at some point in the middle of data collection? Or if working with financials, did the interest calculation change from simple to compound at the end of the year? Does the data distribution stay consistent over all the data? If not, what kinds of actions should be taken to address this problem? Assess the granularity of the data, the range of values, and the level of aggregation of the data.

Does the data represent the population of interest? For marketing data, if the project is focused on targeting customers of child-rearing age, does the data represent that or is it full of senior citizens and teenagers? For time-related variables, are the measurements daily, weekly, monthly? Is that good enough? Is time measured in seconds everywhere? Or is it in milliseconds in some places? Determine the level of granularity of the data needed for the analysis, and assess whether the current level of timestamps on the data meets that need.

Is the data standardized/normalized? Are the scales consistent? If not, how consistent or irregular is the data? These are typical considerations that should be part of the thought process as the team evaluates the datasets that are obtained for the project. Becoming deeply knowledgeable about the data will be critical when it comes time to construct and run models later in the process.

3.3 CHECK THE DATA PORTION OF THE DATASET

setwd("D:/R data")

Employee <- read.csv("Employee.csv")

fix(Employee)

print(Employee)

The print() function lists the contents of the data frame (or any other object). The contents can be changed using the edit() function.

edit(Employee)

3.4 CHECK DIMENSIONALITY OF DATA

Use dim() to obtain the dimensions of the data frame (number of rows and number of columns). The output is a vector.

Dim(Employee)

Use nrow() and ncol() to get the number of rows and number of columns, respectively. We can get the same information by extracting the first and second element of the output vector from dim().

nrow(Employee)

ncol(Employee)

Check the Features and understand the data by printing the first few rows by using the head() function. By default R prints first 6 rows. We can use the head() to obtain the first n observations and tail() to obtain the last n observations; by default, n = 6. These are good commands for obtaining an intuitive idea of what the data look like without revealing the entire data set, which could have millions of rows and thousands of columns.

head(Employee)

If we want to select only a few rows we can specify those number of rows.

Selecting Rows(Observations)

Samp <- Employee[1:3,]

head(mydata) # First 6 rows of dataset

head(mydata, n=10) # First 10 rows of dataset

head(mydata, n= -10) # All rows but the last 10

tail(mydata) # Last 6 rows

tail(mydata, n=10) # Last 10 rows

tail(mydata, n= -10) # All rows but the first 10

Variable names or column names

names(Employee)

3.5 CHECK THE DESCRIPTOR PORTION OF THE DATASET

Descriptor portion means metadata(data about data);

str(Employee)

str() function provides the structure of the data frame. This function identifies the integer and numeric (double) data types, the factor variables and levels, as well as the first few values for each variable. By executing the above code we can obtain information about Variables attributes includes Variable Name, Type etc. "num" denotes that the variable "count" is numeric (continuous), and "Factor" denotes that the variable is categorical with categories or levels.

The command sapply(Employee, class) will return the names and classes (e.g., numeric, integer or character) of each variable within a data frame.

sapply(Employee, class)

To obtain all of the categories or levels of a categorical variable, use the levels() function.

levels(Employee)

3.6 CREATING A VISUALIZATIONS

We commonly use data visualization for data exploration because it allows users to quickly and simply view most of the relevant features of the dataset. Visualizations help us to identify variables that are likely to have interesting relationships. By displaying data graphically through scatter plots or bar charts we can see if two or more variables correlate and determine if they are good candidates for further in-depth analysis. A useful way to perceive patterns and inconsistencies in the data is through the exploratory data analysis with visualization. Visualization gives a concise view of the data that may be difficult to grasp from the numbers and summaries alone. Variables x and y of the data frame data can instead be visualized in a chart or plot which easily depicts the relationship between two variables.

Visualization helps us to create different types of graphs like:

1. Histogram
2. Pie Chart
3. Bar / Line Chart
4. Box plot
5. Scatter plot

Histograms: You can create histograms with the function hist(x) where x is a numeric vector of values to be plotted. The option freq=FALSE plots probability densities instead of frequencies. The option breaks= controls the number of bins.

Simple Histogram

hist(Employee$Salary)

Colored Histogram with Different Number of Bins

hist(Employee$Salary, breaks=12, col="red")

Histograms overlaid

hist(Employee$Salary, breaks="FD", col="green")

hist(Employee$Salary [Employee$Gender=="Male"], breaks="FD", col="gray", add=TRUE)

legend("topright", c("Female","Male"), fill=c("green","gray"))

Pie Charts: Pie charts are created with the function pie(x, labels=) where x is a non-negative numeric vector indicating the area of each slice and labels= notes a character vector of names for the slices.

Simple Pie Chart

Items_sold <- c(10, 12,4, 16, 8)

> *Location <- c("Hyderabad", "Bangalore", "Kolkata", "Mumbai", "Delhi")*
>
> *pie(Items_sold, labels = Location, main="Pie Chart of Locations")*
>
> *# 3D Exploded Pie Chart*
>
> *library(plotrix)*
>
> *pie3D(slices,labels=lbls,explode=0.1, main="Pie Chart of Countries ")*

Bar / Line Chart: Line Chart: Line Charts are commonly preferred when we are to analyze a trend spread over a time period. A line plot is also suitable to plots where we need to compare relative changes in quantities across some variable (like time).

> #To create simple line plot:
>
> Plot(, type=l)

Boxplots: Boxplots can be created for individual variables or for variables by group. The format is boxplot(x, data=), where x is a formula and data= denotes the data frame providing the data. An example of a formula is y~group where a separate boxplot for numeric variable y is generated for each value of the group. Add varwidth=TRUE to make boxplot widths proportional to the square root of the samples sizes. Addhorizontal=TRUE to reverse the axis orientation.

Boxplot of Salary by Education

boxplot(Salary~Education,data=Employee, main="Salary based on Education", xlab="Education", ylab="Salary")

a boxplot is a keyword for generating a boxplot. The plot is done between the Salary of the Employees and the Education Level. The existence of the outliers in the data set is observed as points outside the box.

Scatterplots: There are many ways to create a scatterplot in R. The basic function is a plot(x, y), where x and y are numeric vectors denoting the (x,y) points to plot.

> # Simple Scatterplot
>
> attach(Employee)
>
> plot(Age, Salary, main="Scatterplot on Age vs Salary",
>
> *xlab="Age", ylab="Salary ", pch=19)*

3.7 MISSING DATA

Let us look at how missing data can be detected in the data exploration phase with visualizations. In general, analysts should look for anomalies, verify the data with domain knowledge, and decide the most appropriate approach to clean the data. Consider a scenario in which a bank is conducting data analyses of its account holders to gauge customer retention.

rowSums(is.na(mydata)) # Number of missing per row

colSums(is.na(mydata)) # Number of missing per column/variable

 # Convert to missing data

mydata[mydata$age=="& ",age"] <- NA

mydata[mydata$age==999,"age"] <- NA

 # The function complete.cases() returns a logical vector indicating which cases are complete.

 # list rows of data that have missing values

mydata[!complete.cases(mydata),]

 # The function na.omit() returns the object with listwise deletion of missing values.

 # Creating a new dataset without missing data

mydata1 <- na.omit(mydata)

Extreme Values: The extreme observations are the ones of interest and deserve our attention as being more than just the normal outliers at the end of the bell-curve. These are the ones that skew the distribution into the F-shape shown earlier.

Box Plot for Detecting Outliers: An outlier is a score very different from the rest of the data. When we analyze data we have to be aware of such values because they bias the model we fit the data. A good example of this bias can be seen by looking at a simple statistical model such as mean. Suppose a film gets a rating from 1 to 5. Seven people saw the film and rated the movie with ratings of 2, 5, 4, 5, 5, 5, and 5. All but one of these ratings is fairly similar (mainly 5 and 4) but the first rating was quite different from the rest. It was a rating of 2.

This is an example of an outlier. The box-plots tell us something about the distributions of scores. The boxplots show us the lowest (the bottom horizontal line) and the highest (the top horizontal line). The distance between the lowest horizontal line and the lowest edge of the tinted box is the range between which the lowest 25% of scores fall (called the bottom quartile). The box (the tinted area) shows the middle 50% of scores (known as interquartile range); i.e. 50% of the scores are bigger than the lowest part of the tinted area but smaller than the top part of the tinted area. The distance between the top edge of the tinted box and the top horizontal line shows the range between which top 25% of scores fall (the top quartile). In the middle of the tinted box is a slightly thicker horizontal line. This represents the value of the median.

Like histograms, they also tell us whether the distribution is symmetrical or skewed. For a symmetrical distribution, the whiskers on either side of the box are of equal length. Finally, you will notice small some circles above each boxplot.

These are the cases that are deemed to be outliers. Each circle has a number next to it that tells us in which row of the data editor to find the case. Box-plot is widely used to examine the existence of outliers in the data set. Two important facts that must be kept in mind for box plot are 1. The number of observations in the dataset must be at least as large as five. 2. If there are more than one category in the data set must be sorted according to the category.

A data set containing the marks of 5 students in the subjects English and Science exist in a CSV format. a boxplot is a keyword for generating a boxplot. The plot is done between the marks obtained by the students and the subject. The existence of the outliers in the data set is observed as points outside the box. We want to focus on the interesting moments at the peripheries, known as the outliers and why they could be important. When outliers become extreme observations at either the left or the right it could alter the assumptions made by the statistician at study set-up about the behavior of the recruited population, which could jeopardize the proof of the survey and ultimately expensive failure. The extreme observations are the ones of interest and deserve our attention as being more than just the normal outliers at the end of the bell-curve. These are the ones that skew the distribution into the F-shape.

STEP 4

Data Preparation

4.1 INTRODUCTION

Data preparation includes the steps to explore, preprocess, and complaint data prior to modeling and analysis. Understanding the data in detail is critical to the success of the project. We must decide how to condition and transform data to get it into a format to facilitate subsequent analysis. We may need to perform data visualizations to help us to understand the data, including its trends, outliers, and relationships among data variables. Data preparation tends to be the most labor-intensive step and In fact, it is common for teams to spend at least 50% of a project time in this critical phase. If the team cannot obtain enough data of sufficient quality, it may be unable to perform the subsequent steps in the lifecycle process.

Data Preparation refers to the process of cleaning data, normalizing datasets, and performing transformations on the data. A critical step within the Data Analytics Lifecycle, data conditioning can involve many complex steps to join or merge datasets or otherwise get datasets into a state that enables analysis in further phases. Data conditioning is often viewed as a preprocessing step for the data analysis because it involves many operations on the dataset before developing models to process or analyze the data.

Data preparation steps Includes:

1. Creating New Variables.
2. Grouping Data, Remove duplicate observations in the dataset.
3. Formatting.
4. Keeping, Dropping, Renaming, Labeling.
5. Conditional Processing.
6. Functions.
7. Combining Datasets.
8. Transposing Data.

4.2 CREATING NEW VARIABLES

Let us take Employees dataset, we have their monthly Income details, we want to calculate their Salary hike and compute New Salary.

We use the assignment operator (<-) to create new variables.

setwd("D:/R data")

Employee <- read.csv("Employee.csv")

fix(Employee)

Create a variable called Bonus with 8% increase in the salary

Employee$Bonus <- Employee$Salary.08*

Employee$Newsal <- Employee$Salary + Employee$Bonus

fix(Employee)

4.3 SORTING DATA

To Group a data frame in R, use the order( ) function. By default, sorting is ASCENDING. Prepend the sorting variable. By a minus sign to indicate DESCENDING order.

```
# Sort by Age
Agesort <- Employee[order(Age),]
#Sorting with Multiple Variables, sort by Gender and Age
Mul_sort <- Employee[order(Gender, Age),]
```

By executing the above code we sorted the data frame based on Gender as first preference and Age as second.

```
#Sort by Gender (ascending) and Age (descending)
Rev_sort <- Employee[order(Gender, -Age),]
detach(Employee)
```

4.4 IDENTIFYING AND REMOVING DUPLICATED DATA

We can remove duplicate data using functions duplicated() and unique() as well as the function distinct in dplyr package. The function duplicated() returns a logical vector where TRUE specifies which elements of a vector or data frame are duplicates.

Given the following vector:

Cust_Id <- c(101, 104, 104, 105, 104, 105)

To find the position of duplicate elements in x, we can use this:

duplicated(Cust_Id)

We can print the duplicate elements by executing the following code.

Cust_Id [duplicated(Cust_Id)]

If you want to remove duplicated elements and to get only unique values use !duplicated(), where ! is a logical negation:

Uniq_Cust<- Cust_Id [!duplicated(Cust_Id)]

In our day to day tasks, we need to create, modify, manipulate, and transform data in order to make the data ready for Analysis and Reporting. We use some or other Function for most data manipulations. Familiarity with these functions can make programming much easier. We can remove duplicate rows from a data frame based on column values, as follow: # Remove duplicates based on Work_Balance columns

Uniq_WB <- Employee [!duplicated(Employee$ Work_Balance),]

You can extract unique elements as follow:

unique(Cust_Id)

It's also possible to apply unique() on a data frame, for removing duplicated rows as follow:

unique(Employee)

The function distinct() in dplyr package can be used to keep only unique/distinct rows from a data frame. If there are duplicate rows, only the first row is preserved. It's an efficient version of the R base function unique().

The dplyr package can be loaded and installed as follow:

install.packages("dplyr")

library("dplyr")

Remove duplicate rows based on all columns:

distinct(Employee)

#Remove duplicate rows based on certain columns (variables): Remove duplicated rows based on JobSatisfaction.

distinct(Employee, JobSatisfaction)

Remove duplicated rows based on JobSatisfaction and Perf_Rating.

distinct(Employee, JobSatisfaction, Perf_Rating)

4.5 FILTERING THE OBSERVATIONS BASED ON CONDITIONS

Age_Con <- Employee[which(Employee$Age < 40),]

While filtering observations based on character variables we need embed the string in quotes.

Sex_Con <- Employee[which(Employee$Gender ="male"),]

Filter the Observations based on multiple conditions

Mul_Con <-Employee[which(Employee $Gender=='Female' & Employee $Age < 30),]

Selection using the Subset Function

The subset( ) function is the easiest way to select variables and observations. In the following example, we select all rows that have a value of age greater than or equal to 50 or age less than 30. We keep the Emp_Id and Age columns.

#Using subset function

Test <- subset(Employee, Age >= 50 | Age < 30, select=c(Emp_Id, Age))

Conditional Processing:

Quite often we need to process data based on certain conditions, and decision making is an important part of programming. This can be achieved by using the conditional if...else statement.

If Statement Syntax:

if (test_expression) {

statement

}

We can Create new variables using if then else. We want to promote our product to only those people whose income is more than 40K.

Employee$Promo <- ifelse(Employee$Salary>40000,"Promote Product","Do not Promote Product")

fix(Employee)

#Here, We check to see if the elements of Employee$Salary are greater than 40000 if an element is greater than 40000, it assigns the value of Promote Product to Employee$Promo, and if it's not greater than 40000, it assigns the value of Do not Promote Product to Employee$Promo.

We want to assign values Low, Medium, and High to a Sal_Grp variable. To do this, we can use nested ifelse() statements:

Employee$Sal_Grp <-ifelse(Employee$Salary >20000 & Employee$Salary<50000," Medium",

ifelse(Employee$Salary >= 50000, "High","Low"))

Now this says, first check whether each element of the Salary vector is >20000 and <50000. If it is, assign Medium to Sal_Grp. If it's not, then evaluate the next ifelse() statement, whether Salary>50000. If it is, assign Sal_Grp a value of High. If it's not any of those, then assign it Low.

4.6 FORMATTING

This is commonly used to improve the appearance of output, we can use already existing(System-defined) formats and even create custom formats to bin values in an efficient way. By using this, we can group data in different ways without having to create a new data set. Let us Imagine, we conducted a survey on a New Product (A/c): Overall satisfied - 1 - Vey low 2- Low 3. OK, 4- Good 5- extremely Good. While there are many ways to write custom solutions, the analyst should be familiar with special-purpose procedures that can reduce the need for custom coding. R will treat factors as nominal variables and ordered factors as ordinal variables. You can use options in the factor() and ordered ( ) functions to control the mapping of integers to strings.

We can use the factor function to create your own value labels.

setwd("D:/R data")

Shop <- read.csv("Shopping.csv")

fix(Shop)

Brand variable in Shop dataset is coded 1, 2, 3.: We want to attach value labels 1=Samsung, 2=Hitachi, 3=Bluestar.

Shop$Brand <- factor(Shop$Brand, levels = c(1,2,3),

labels = c("Samsung", "Hitachi", "Bluestar"))

variable y is coded 1,2, 3,4 and 5 # we want to attach value labels 1 - Vey low 2- Low 3. OK 4- Good 5- extremely Good.

Shop$Overall_Sat <- ordered(Shop$Overall_Sat, levels = c(1,2,3,4,5),

labels = c("Very Low", "Low", "OK", "Good", "Extremely Good"))

Sometimes you may want to create a new categorical variable by classifying the observations according to the value of a continuous variable. Suppose that you want to create a new variable called Age.Cat, which classifies the people as "Young", "Adult", and "Old" according to their Age. People less than 35 years are classified as Young, people between 35 and 60 are classified as Adult, and people greater than 60 are classified as Old.

Employee$Age.Cat<-cut(Employee$Age, c(18,35, 60,90), c("Young", "Adult", "Old"))

4.7 KEEPING, DROPPING, RENAMING, LABELLING

Select variables

myvars <- c("Brand", "Safety", "Look")

Sub_shop <- Shop[myvars]

fix(Sub_shop)

Exclude 4th and 6th variable

Sub_data <- Shop[c(-4,-6)]

fix(Sub_data)

Rename interactively

fix(Shop) # results are saved on close

Rename programmatically

library(reshape)

Ren_Shop <- rename(Shop, c(Safety="Security"))

Labeling the Variables: We can assign the variable labels in var.labels to the columns in the data frame data using the function label from the Hmisc package.

install.packages("Hmisc")

library("Hmisc")

label(Shop[["Overall_Sat"]]) <- "Overall Satisfaction of the Customer"

label(Shop[["Look"]]) <- "Look and Feel of the Product"

label(Shop)

4.8 FUNCTIONS

A Function returns a value from a computation or system manipulation that requires zero or more arguments. The function is created by using the keyword function.

The basic syntax of an R function definition is as follows:

New_Var <- Function_Name(Argument1, Argument2,...N).

Function recognized in by the use of a function name, followed immediately by function argument(s), separated by commas, and enclosed in parentheses. However, the number of required and optional arguments varies. Some functions simply have one required argument. Others have one required and one or more optional arguments. In most cases, the order of the arguments is important. Some functions take no arguments, in which case a null set of parentheses is required.

Character Functions:

toupper, tolower Functions: These functions change the case of the argument.

Name <- 'Ramya Kalidindi' #Assigning a value to a variable

upcf <- toupper (Name)

locf <- tolower(Name)

trimws Function: Quite often, the data we receive might contain unwanted spaces, and we want to remove them to make our data clean. We use trimws function to deal with blanks of a string.

Name <- " Y Lakshmi Prasad "

Trimmed_Name <- trimws(Name, which = c("both", "left", "right"))

substr Function: This function is used to Extract characters from string variables. The arguments to substr() specify the input vector, start character position and end character position. The last parameter is optional. When omitted, all characters after the location specified in the second space will be extracted.

Req_Name <- substr(Name, 6, 12)

Create string variables from numeric variables

stringx <- as.character(numericx)

typeof(stringx)

typeof(numericx)

The typeof() function can be used to verify the type of an object, possible values include logical, integer, double, complex, character, raw, list, NULL, closure (function), special and built in.

Create numeric variables from string variables: The argument in as.numeric function, integer is the number of characters in the string, while decimal is an optional specification of how many characters appear after the decimal.

numericx <- as.numeric(stringx)

typeof(stringx)

typeof(numericx)

Task: Calculate increment at 10% and derive new salary for each Id.

Num_data <- data.frame(Id = c(101,102,103),

   Salary =c(40700,12000,37000))

sapply(Num_data, mode)

Num_data$Char_sal <- as.character(Num_data$Salary)

typeof(Num_data$Char_sal)

Num_data$Saln <- as.numeric(Num_data$Char_sal)

typeof(Num_data$Saln)

Num_data$Bonus <- Num_data$Saln*.10

fix(Num_data)

Num_data$New_Sal <- Num_data$Saln+Num_data$Bonus

Numeric Functions:

Abs Function: We use this function to Obtain the absolute value;

a=5

aba <- abs(a)

Val <- -28.86

Req <- abs(Val))

Floor(Base) and ceiling(Top) values:

X=43.837 #This value lies between 43 and 44

Flx=floor(X) #Base value

Cilx=ceiling(X) #Top value

Round Function:

Val= 43.837

Rval1=round(Val) #44

Rval2=round(Val,digits=2) #43.84

MAX Function: Returns the Largest non-missing value from the list

X=max(2,6,NA,8,0)

Min Function: Returns the Smallest non missing value from the list

Y=min(2,6,1,7,0,-2)

Sum Function: It Returns the Sum (Total) of values

Y=Sum(9,8,.,9)

Mean Function: It is calculated by taking the sum of the values and dividing with the number of values in a data series. The function mean() is used to calculate this in R.

Create a vector and find its mean.

x <- c(7,3,NA,4,18,2,54,8)

res_mean <- mean(x)

print(res_mean)

Find mean dropping NA values.

resmean_na <- mean(x,na.rm = TRUE)

print(resmean_na)

Median Function: The middle most value in a data series is called the median. The median()function is used in R to calculate this value.

Create the vector and Find the median.

x <- c(12,7,3,4.2,18,2,54,-21,8,-5)

median.result <- median(x)

print(median.result)

Date/Time Functions: Date/Time functions are a set of functions that return portions of date time, date, or time values or convert numeric values into R date or time values. These functions are useful for extracting the date and time from a date time value or converting separate month, day and year values into a R date value.

Sys.Date, date Functions: These function returns today's date from the system clock, requiring No Arguments.

Sys.Date( ) returns today's date.

date() returns the current date and time.

print today's date

today <- Sys.Date()

format(today, format="%B %d %Y")

format(today, format="%m %d %Y")

format(today, format="%m %d %y")

You can observe that the system date is presented in different ways as we change the format. We need to find what format matches better to our requirement and go for it.

Converting Character to Date: You can use the as.Date( ) function to convert character data to dates. The format is as.Date(x,"format"), where x is the character data and format gives the appropriate format.

The default format is yyyy-mm-dd

Testdts <- as.Date(c("1982-07-12", "1975-03-01"))

Use as.Date( ) to convert strings to dates

Testdts <- as.Date(c("1982-07-12", "1975-03-01"))

number of days between 7/12/82 and 03/01/75

days <- Testdts [1] - Testdts [2]

4.9 COMBINING DATASETS

Reading data from two or more data sets and processing them by Append Rows, Append Columns, Merging.

Appending Rows: Concatenating datasets essentially means stacking one dataset on top of the other, that is, given two datasets, all of the records from the second dataset will be added to the end of the first dataset when concatenating datasets we would expect the datasets to have identical structure but different contents. By structure, we mean the tables would have the same columns names and the columns would have the same type (numeric or character). If a column exists in one or more of the datasets but not in another, that column is included in all of the output records but with a missing value for all of the records in the table(s) that did not have that column.

The rbind function allows you to attach one dataset to the bottom of the other, which is known as appending or concatenating the datasets. This is useful when you want to combine two datasets that contain different observations for the same variables. When using the rbind function, We need to make sure that each dataset contains the same number of variables and all of the variable names match. You may need to remove or rename some variables in the process. The variables need not be arranged in the same order within the datasets, as the rbind function automatically matches them by name. The rbind function does not identify duplicates or sort the data. You can do this with the unique and order functions.

> *sale1 <- data.frame(Cust_Id = c(101,103,105),*
>
> > *Amount_Spent =c(1700,1200,3700),*
> >
> > *Pur_dt = c(20-03-2015,20-03-2015,20-03-2015))*
>
> *fix(sale1)*
>
> *sale2 <- data.frame(Cust_Id = c(103,104,105,108),*
>
> > *Pur_dt = c(22-03-2015,22-03-2015,22-03-2015,22-03-2015),*
> >
> > *Amount_Spent =c(1800,3400,2500,3200))*
>
> *fix(sale2)*
>
> *saleall <-rbind(sale1, sale2)*
>
> *fix(saleall)*

Notice that the new dataset contains all of the original data in the original order, including two copies of the data for Cust_Id 103 and 105. We can append two or more datasets in the same manner.

Appending Columns: The cbind function pastes one dataset to the side of another. This is useful if the data from corresponding rows of each dataset belong to the same observation. You can only use the cbind function to combine datasets that have the same number of rows.

Merging Datasets by Common Variables: The merge function allows you to combine two datasets by matching the observations according to the values of common variables. Consider the sale1 and loc1 datasets. The datasets have a common variable called Cust_Id, which can be used to match corresponding observations.

> *loc1 <- data.frame(Cust_Id = c(101,102,103,104,105),*
>
> > *Location =c("Hyderabad","Bangalore","Chennai","Hyderabad","Bangalore"))*
>
> *Merdata <- merge(sale1,loc1)*
>
> *fix(Merdata)*

The merge function identifies variables with the same name and uses them to match up the observations. In this example, both datasets contain a variable named Cust_Id, so R automatically uses this variable to match the observations.

> *All_mer <- merge(sale1,loc1,all=T)*
>
> *fix(All_mer)*

When you combine two datasets with the merge function, R automatically excludes any unmatched observations that appear in only one of the datasets. The all, all.x, and all.y arguments allow you to control how R deals with any unmatched observations. To keep all unmatched observations, set the all argument to T:

L_mer <- merge(sale1,loc1,all.x=T)

fix(L_mer)

R_mer <- merge(sale1,loc1,all.y=T)

fix(R_mer)

To merge two data frames (datasets) horizontally, use the merge function. In most cases, you join two data frames by one or more common key variables (i.e., an inner join).

 # merge two data frames by ID

total <- merge(data frameA,data frameB,by="ID")

Adding Rows: To join two data frames (datasets) vertically, use the rbind function. The two data frames must have the same variables, but they do not have to be in the same order.

total <- rbind(data frameA, data frameB)

4.10 TRANSPOSING THE DATASETS

Reshaping a dataset is also known as Rotating, Transposing or Transforming a dataset. It usually applies to datasets in which repeat measurements have been taken, reshape function is used to change the data orientation., But prior to performing reshaping we need to ask ourselves these following questions:

- ◆ What should stay same
- ◆ Which variable should go up
- ◆ Which variable should go down
- ◆ Which variable should go to the middle

#Transposing Data

setwd("D:/R data")

Vitals <- read.csv("Vitals.csv")

fix(Vitals)

T_vitals<-reshape(Vitals, direction="wide", v.names="Result", timevar="VS_Test", idvar="Pat_Id")

fix(T_vitals)

Since Pat_Id is specified in idvar it remained at the same position, all the other variables transposed. Use the v.names argument to specify the variable that you want to separate into different columns. Use the timevar argument to specify the variable that indicates which column the value belongs to. Use the idvar argument to specify which variable is used to group the records together.

STEP 5

Statistical Thinking

5.1 INTRODUCTION

Statistics is the science that deals with the collection, Classification, analysis and Interpretation of numerical facts and the use of probability theory to impose order on aggregates of data. Let us look at some Business Problems faced by a Business Man, where he needs Statistical Methods to solve them.

- Where should we open our new retail store?
- How big the premises Should we rent?
- How many people should I staff for this store?
- What is the right level of inventory for each product?
- How to increase customer value and overall revenues?
- How to develop successful new products?
- Should we accept online orders or not?
- How much should we invest in advertising?
- How to reduce operational cost?

5.2 STATISTICAL TERMINOLOGY

Prior to solving the above-mentioned problems let us look at some statistical terms which make us comfortable to deal with these scenarios.

Population: Population is a complete set of Items that share at least one property in common.

Sample: A subset of the population that is selected for analysis.

Parameter: A measure that is calculated on the entire population.

Statistics: A measure that is calculated on the sample.

Descriptive Statistics: These are used to describe or summarize data in ways that are meaningful and useful. We can describe data in many ways like measures of central tendency, Measures of dispersion, measures of location and shape of the distribution. Descriptive Measures gives a better sense of data and can present an overall picture of the data, these statistics include Mean, Mode, Median, Minimum, Maximum, Variance, Standard deviation, Skewness, Kurtosis etc.

Inferential Statistics: Methods that employ probability theory for deducing the properties of a population from the analysis of the properties of a data sample drawn from it.

Predictive Statistics: Methods concerned with predicting future probabilities based on historical data.

Prescriptive Statistics: Methods allow us to prescribe a number of possible actions and guide us towards an optimal solution.

Random Variable: A variable whose value is subject to variation due to chance.

Bias: Giving unfair preference to one thing against the other.

Variable: Variable is a characteristic or attribute that can be measured or counted.

Data can be classified into 2 Types:

1. **Qualitative Data:** If we can set the data into any number of groups, we call that data as Qualitative data. If there is no ordering between the categories we call that variable as Nominal variable, if the categories may be ordered then we call that variable as an ordinal variable.

2. **Quantitative Data:** It is a measurement expressed in numbers, but not all numbers are quantitative like, mobile number and postal code in India, which we cannot add or subtract.

5.3 SCALES OF MEASUREMENT

These are ways to categorize different types of variables.

Nominal Scale: This scale satisfies the identity property of measurement. Let us take Gender as an example, Individuals may be classified as "male" or "female", but neither value represents more or less "gender" than the other. Religion and race are other examples of variables that are normally measured on a nominal scale.

Ordinal Scale: This scale has the property of both identity and magnitude. Each value on the ordinal scale has a unique meaning, and it has an ordered relationship to every other value on the scale. Let us take the example of how do you rate the movie?. We get responses of Very good, good, Average, Bad etc,

Interval Scale: This scale has the properties of identity, magnitude, and equal intervals. A perfect example of an interval scale is the Fahrenheit scale to measure temperature. The scale is made up of equal temperature units so that the difference between 40 and 50 degrees Fahrenheit is equal to the difference between 50 and 60 degrees Fahrenheit. With an interval scale, you also know how much bigger or smaller they are.

Ratio Scale: This scale of measurement satisfies all four of the properties of measurement: identity, magnitude, equal intervals, and an absolute zero. For example, if the weight of an object is 80 kilograms we can say that this object is double to an object weighs 40 kilograms. Variables like Height, Age, Weight has a unique meaning, can be rank ordered, units along the scale are equal to one another, and there is an absolute zero.

5.4 SAMPLING TECHNIQUES

Sampling techniques are the methods used to draw a sample from the population. There are different methods for sampling. A sample statistic is a characteristic of the sample, sample statistics might be used as a point estimate for a population parameter.

Selecting a Simple Random Sample (SRS):

- Unbiased: Each unit has equal chance of being chosen in the sample
- Independent: Selection of one unit has no influence on selection of other units
- SRS is a gold standard against which all other samples are measured

Selecting the Sampling Frame:

- Sampling frame is simply a list of items from which to draw a sample.
- Does the sampling frame represent the population?
- The available list may differ from the desired list: e.g. we don't have list of customers who did not buy from a store.
- Sometimes, no comprehensive sampling frame exists: When forecasting for the future. Thus a comprehensive list of acceptances of credit card offers does not exist yet.

Typical Downsides in Sampling:

- Collecting data only from volunteers (voluntary response sample): – e.g. online reviews (maps.google.com, tripadvisor.com)
- Picking easily available respondents (convenience sample): – e.g. choosing to survey in In-Orbit mall
- A high rate of non-response (more than 70%): – e.g. CEO / CIO surveys on some industry trends

Sampling variation:

- Sample mean varies from one sample to another
- Sample mean can be (and most likely is) different from the population mean
- Sample mean is a random variable

Central Limit Theorem (CLT) & the distribution of the sample mean:

The distribution of the sample mean will be normal when the distribution of data in the population is normal. Otherwise, we assume it to be approximately normal even if the distribution of data in the population is not normal if the sample size is "fairly large". CLT is Valid When each data point in the sample is independent of the other and the sample size is large enough.

How Large is Large Enough?

- It depends on distribution of data – primarily its symmetry and presence of outliers
- If data is quite symmetric and has few outliers, even smaller samples are fine. Otherwise, we need larger samples
- A sample size of 30 is considered large enough, but that may/ may not be adequate

Sampling Distributions and the Central Limit Theorem:

- How many new customers will I acquire if I open a store in this area?
- What is the right level of inventory for What is the right level of inventory for our new e-reader?
- What is the impact of a stock-out on What is the impact of a stock-out on consumer behavior?
- What interest rate should we charge for this loan?
- Will our quality improve after the consulting assignment?
- What is the amount of time spent by our potential customers on the web?
- Have our order lead times gone down after the merger?
- How many such loans have How many such loans have defaulted in the past?
- What is the amount of person-hours required to complete such a project?

Introduction To Probability Theory: Probability is used throughout business to evaluate decision-making risks. Every decision made by us carries some chance for failure, so probability analysis is conducted formally and informally.

Most of us use probabilities with two conditions:

1. When one event or another will occur
2. Where two or more events will both occur

Let us understand this from a Jewelry mart example, on a Festival Day. What is the probability that today's demand will exceed our average sales? What is the probability that demand will exceed our average sales and that more than 20% of our sales force will not report for work?

Random Variable:

- A random variable describes the probabilities for an uncertain future numerical outcome of a random process.
- It is a variable because it can take one of the several possible values.
- It is random because there is some chance associated with each possible value.

Independent: When the value taken by one random variable does not affect the value taken by the other random variable: e.g. Roll of two dice.

Dependent: When the value of one random variable gives us more information about the other random variable: e.g. Height and weight of students.

5.5 PROBABILITY THEORY

Classical Approach: Probability of an event is equal to Number of outcomes where the event occurs divided by a total number of possible outcomes.

Relative Frequency Approach: When tossing a coin, initially the ratio of a number of heads to a number of trials will remain volatile. As the number of trials increases, the ratio converges to a fixed number (say 0.5).

Subjective Probability Approach: It is based on individual's past experience and intuition. Most managerial decisions are concerned with specific, unique situations.

Probability Distribution: A probability distribution is a rule that identifies possible outcomes of a random variable and assigns a probability to each.

- A discrete distribution has a finite number of values: e.g. face value of a card, work experience of students rounded off to the nearest month.
- A continuous distribution has all possible values in some range: e.g. sales per month in a retail store, heart rate of patients in the hospital. Continuous distributions are nicer to deal with and are good approximations when there are a large number of possible values

Discrete Probability Distribution: Suppose you randomly picked a card from the card deck. What is the probability that this card will be

- Bigger than 7?
- Equal to or bigger than 6?
- Smaller than 3?
- Greater than 4 and less than 8?

The daily sales of large flat-panel TVs at a store (X): What is the probability of a sale? What is the probability of selling at least three TVs?

Expected Value or Mean: The expected value or mean (μ) of a random variable is the weighted average of its values, the probabilities serve as weights. What is the mean number of Watches sold per day?

Variance and Standard Deviation: Both measures of variation or uncertainty in the random variable.

Variance ($\sigma2$): The weighted average of the squared deviations from the mean, Probabilities serve as weights, Units are square of the units of the variable.

Standard deviation (σ): Square root of variance, Have same units as the variable

Binomial Distribution: The binomial distribution describes discrete data resulting from an experiment known as Bernoulli process. The tossing of a fair coin a fixed number of times is a Bernoulli process and the outcomes of such tosses can be represented by the binomial probability distribution. The success or failure of interviewees on an aptitude test may also be described by a Bernoulli process. On the other hand, the frequency distribution of the lives of fluorescent lights in a factory would be measured on a continuous scale of hours and would not qualify as a binomial distribution. The probability mass function, the mean, and the variance are as follows:

Characteristics of a Binomial Distribution

- There can be only two possible outcomes: heads or tails, yes or no, success or failure
- Each Bernoulli process has its own characteristic probability. Take the situation in which historically seven – tenths of all people who applied for a certain type of job passed the job test. We would say that the characteristic probability here is 0.7, but we could describe our testing results as Bernoulli only if we felt certain that the proportion of those passing the test (0.07) remained constant over time.
- At the same time, the outcome of one test must not affect the outcome of the other tests.

Poisson Distribution: The Poisson distribution is used to describe a number of processes, including the distribution of telephone calls going through a switchboard system, the demand of patients for service at a health institution, the arrivals of trucks and cars at a toll booth, and the number of accidents at an intersection.

These examples all have a common element: They can be described by a discrete random variable that takes on integer values (0, 1, 2, 3, 4, and so on). The number of patients who arrive at a hospital in a given interval of time will be 0, 1, 2, 3, 4, 5, or some other whole number. Similarly, if you count the number of cars arriving at a tollbooth on a highway during some 10 minutes period, the number will be 0, 1, 2, 3, 4, 5, and so on.

The probability mass function, the mean, and the variance are as follows:

Characteristics of a Poisson Distribution

- If we consider the example of a number of cars, then the average number of vehicles that arrive per rush hour can be estimated from the past traffic data.
- If we divide the rush hour into intervals of one second each, we will find the following statements to be true.
- The probability that exactly one vehicle will arrive at the single booth per second is a very small number and is constant for every one-second interval.
- The probability that two or more vehicles will arrive within the one-second interval is so small that we can assign it a zero value.

- The number of vehicles that arrive in a given one-second interval is independent of the time at which that one-second interval occurs during the rush hour.
- The number of arrivals in any one-second interval is not dependent on the number of arrivals in any other one-second interval.

5.6 NORMAL DISTRIBUTION

What is a Normal Distribution?

- How to do probability calculations associated with normal distribution?
- What are various important properties of the normal distribution?

Basics of Normal Distribution:

- The graph of the pdf (probability density function) is a bell shaped curve
- The normal random variable takes values from - ∞ to +∞
- It is symmetric and centered around the mean (which is also the median and mode)
- Any normal distribution can be specified with just two parameters – the mean (μ) and the standard deviation (σ)
- We write this as $X \sim N(\mu, \sigma2)$

The normal distribution has applications in many areas of business administration. For example:

- Modern portfolio theory commonly assumes that the returns of a diversified asset portfolio follow a normal distribution.
- In operations management, process variations often are normally distributed.
- In human resource management, employee performance sometimes is considered to be normally distributed.

Is The Distribution Normal? The following conditions should be satisfied by the distribution in order to be a normal distribution:

- The mean, median and mode should be almost equal
- The standard deviation should be low
- Skewness and kurtosis should be close to zero
- Median should lie exactly in between the upper and lower quartile

Normal Probability Plot: The normal probability plot is a graphical technique for normality testing: assessing whether or not a data set is approximately normally distributed. Here we are basically comparing the observed cumulative probability with the theoretical cumulative probability. If the observed data are really from the normal distribution, then we should get a straight line.

For a normal distribution, 68.2% of the data lies within the one standard deviation range. (mean - standard deviation, mean + standard deviation).

Departures from Normality: How can we say that the normal distribution is a reasonable approximation of the data? We can look at the data 1. More than one mode suggesting data come from distinct groups, 2. Data Lacks symmetry, 3.Unusual extreme values. If any of these observed we can say that the data is not normal. We Can identify these differences by looking at 1.Visual inspection of the histogram 2.Numerical summaries like Skewness and Kurtosis 3. Graphical summaries (Normal Quantile plot).

1. **Measures of central tendency:** There are precisely three ways to find the central value: Arithmetic mean, Median and Mode.

   Mean or average, is calculated by finding the sum of the study data and dividing it by the total number of data. Determining the heart rate is an important part of the medical condition. Here's a vector containing the number of heart beats.

   beats <- c(94, 83, 84, 93, 82, 78, 98, 84)

   A quick way to assess our this data would be to get the average of the beats. Statisticians call this the "mean". Call the mean function with the beats vector.

   > *mean (beats)*

   > *barplot(beats)*

   If we draw a line on the plot representing the mean, we can easily compare the various values to the average. The **abline** function can take an h parameter with a value at which to draw a horizontal line or a v parameter for a vertical line. When it's called, it updates the previous plot.

   Draw a horizontal line across the plot at the mean:

   > *abline(h=mean(beats))*

   The median is the middle value in a set of data. It is calculated by first arranging the data in numerical order then locate the value in the middle of the list. Let's take the example of marks obtained by a group of students. Assume that the exam been conducted for 50 marks.

   > *marks <- c(14, 13, 14, 23, 42, 24, 47, 18)*

   > *mean(marks)*

   Let's see how this new mean shows up on our same graph.

   > *barplot(marks)*

   > *abline(h = mean(marks))*

   It may be factually accurate to say that our students have an average of 24.375 marks, but it's probably also misleading. For situations like this, it's probably more useful to talk about the "median" value. The median is calculated by sorting the values and choosing the middle one.

   Call the median function on the vector:

   > *median(marks)*

Let's show the median on the plot. Draw a horizontal line across the plot at the median.

> *abline (h=median(marks))*

The mode is the number that appears most frequently in the set of data.

2. **Measures of Dispersion:** We even want to find out how to spread out the data is from the central value i.e. mean. In this case, we would like to have a look at measures of dispersion like Range, Variance, Standard Deviation.

   Range: To obtain range you subtract the smallest number from the largest number.

   Variance: It comes from the sum of squared difference of the each data from the arithmetic mean of the data.

   Standard Deviation: Take the square root of the variance, we get the Standard Deviation of the data. Statisticians use the concept of "standard deviation" from the mean to describe the range of typical values for a data set. For a group of numbers, it shows how much they typically vary from the average value. To calculate the standard deviation, you calculate the mean of the values, then subtract the mean from each number and square the result, then average those squares, and take the square root of that average.

   Take a vector with the values of salaries of people working in a department.

   salary <- c(46000, 50000, 35000, 30000, 44800, 45000, 10200, 15000)

   barplot(salary)

   meanValue <- mean(salary)

   Let's see a plot showing the mean value:

   abline(h=meanValue)

   To calculate standard deviation we use **sd** function. Let us call **sd** on the salary vector now, and assign the result to the deviation variable.

   deviation <- sd(salary)

   We'll add a line on the plot to show one standard deviation above the mean

   abline(h = meanValue + deviation)

   Now try adding a line on the plot to show one standard deviation below the mean (the bottom of the normal range):

   abline(h = meanValue - deviation)

3. **Measures of Location:** To understand the data better, we observe even measures of a location like quartiles, deciles and percentiles which make the data into 4, 10 and 100 parts respectively.

4. **The shape of the distribution**: There are two statistics related to the shape, Skewness, and Kurtosis.

   Skewness: It detects whether the data is symmetric about the central value of the distribution. If the histogram has a long left tail we call the data is

Negatively skewed, and if the histogram has long right tail we can say that the data positively skewed.

Kurtosis: It is a measure that can say about how flat or peaked the data is. If the value of kurtosis is positive we can understand that the data is leptokurtic(Peaked), if the value is negative the data is platykurtic(Flat). The value of kurtosis for a Mesokurtic Distribution is zero(Normal).

Normal distribution is asymmetric, a continuous probability distribution that is uniquely specified by a mean and standard deviation. Every normal distribution can be converted into a standard normal distribution (Z-score).

5.7 OBTAINING DESCRIPTIVE STATISTICS

To calculate a particular statistic for each of the variables in a dataset simultaneously, use the sapply function if the dataset has any missing values then set the **na.rm** argument to T:

sapply(Health, mean, na.rm=T)

We can observe some warnings in the console window this is because, If any of the variables in your dataset are non-numeric, the sapply function behaves inconsistently. Here we attempt to calculate the maximum value for each of the variables in the Health dataset. R returns an error message because the few variables in the dataset are factor variables. To avoid this problem, exclude any non-numeric variables from the dataset by using bracket subset function.

If we want to group the values of a numeric variable according to the levels of a factor and calculate a statistic for each group, we can use tapply or aggregate functions.

tapply(Health$Age, Health$Gender, mean)

We can also use the aggregate function to summarize variables by groups. Using the aggregate function has the advantage that you can summarize several continuous variables simultaneously.

aggregate(Employee$Salary~Gender, Employee, mean)

Again, you can also use more than one grouping variable. For example, to calculate the mean of salary for each combination of gender and education for the Employee dataset:

aggregate(Salary~Gender+Education, Employee, mean)

To summarize two or more continuous variables simultaneously, nest them inside the cbind function.

aggregate(cbind(Salary,Age)~Level, Employee, mean)

Obtain Cross-tabular frequency: Cross tabulation or contingency table is a type of table that displays the frequency distribution of the variables on the row and the other on the column. These tables are widely used in Business Analytics since they provide interrelations between variables.

Let us build contingency table by using table function on the Health$Gender and Health$Response factors

You can generate frequency tables using the **table( )** function, tables of proportions using the **prop.table( )** function, and marginal frequencies using **margin.table( )**.

 # build a contingency table based on the Gender and Response factors

Health_table <- table(Health$Gender,Health$Response)

Health_table

margin.table(Health_table, 1) # A frequencies (summed over B)

margin.table(Health_table, 2) # B frequencies (summed over A)

prop.table(Health_table) # cell percentages

prop.table(Health_table, 1) # row percentages

prop.table(Health_table, 2) # column percentages

Summary Function: The summary() function provides several descriptive statistics, such as the mean and median, about a variable such as Height in Health data frame. To produce a summary of all the variables in a dataset, use the summary function. The function summarizes each variable in a manner suitable for its class. For numeric variables, it gives the mean, median, range, and interquartile range. For factor variables, it gives the number in each category. If a variable has any missing values, it will tell you how many missing values are there.

summary(Health) will provide an overview of the distribution of each column.

The **summary** function generates all the descriptive statistics associated with the variable height in the data set Health. Normality of a distribution implies an element of symmetry associated with the distribution. The Skewness and Kurtosis of the data set occurs in the neighborhood of zero. A basic analysis yields the result that the variable height is normally distributed in the data set Health.

5.8 OBTAINING INFERENTIAL STATISTICS

Inferential Statistics refers to Drawing conclusions about the population based on sample data.

Confidence Intervals: While performing Statistical Analysis we need to answer the following questions.

- ◆ How to provide an interval estimate (confidence interval) for population parameters such as mean?
- ◆ How to adjust the interval estimate if the population standard deviation is not known?
- ◆ How to calculate confidence interval for population proportion?

♦   What should be the sample size to collect for a desired width of the interval estimate?

Hypothesis Testing:

1.   Should I staff this project with one more programmer?
2.   Should we open our new retail store at location X?
3.   Should we hire this consulting company?
4.   Should we acquire this airline?
5.   Should we invest in online advertising?
6.   Should we increase the interest rate for this loan?
7.   Should we enter the Indian retail market?

When we are solving these sort of questions, we may need to find out answers for some more questions like:

♦   How and when to formulate hypotheses about population parameters?
♦   How to quantify the strength of the evidence?
♦   What are Type I and Type II errors?

How to frame hypothesis: Hypothesis is a starting position that is open to a test and rejection in light of strong adverse evidence. The initial belief is called the null hypothesis (H0) Generally the status quo it says Do nothing. Its negation is called the alternative hypothesis (HA, Ha, H1) Often a claim to be tested, or a change to be detected it says Do something. The two hypotheses are Mutually exclusive and Collectively exhaustive

Hypothesis-Testing Process: Start with Hypotheses about a Population Parameter. The parameter could be mean, proportion or something else. Collect information from a randomly chosen sample and calculate the appropriate sample statistic. We Reject/ Do Not Reject Hypothesis based on the sample information if it is strongly inconsistent with the null hypothesis? If yes then the rejected hypothesis.

Supermarket Loyalty Program Example: A supermarket plans to launch a loyalty program if it results in an average spending per shopper of more than $120 per week. A random sample of 80 shoppers enrolled in the pilot program spent an average of $130 in a week with a standard deviation of $40.Should the loyalty program be launched?

The Testing Process

• Begin by assuming that H0 (typically status quo) is true?: e.g. I believe that the spending will be less than or equal to $120.
• Quantify what is meant by "strong enough evidence" to reject H0: e.g. Probability of finding a sample mean should be less than 0.05
• Collect the evidence that would be used to test H0:e.g. A pilot resulted in average spending of $130 in a sample of 80 customers

- Calculate the probability of observing the given or stronger evidence, e.g. The maximum probability of getting a sample of $130 or more under H0 is 0.01
- Conclude and take appropriate action? :e.g. The evidence is strong enough (0.01 < 0.05) to reject H0, then launch the card.

While making the conclusions, you can make two types of errors:

Decision/Reality	Do not reject H0	Reject H0
H0 is true	Correct decision	Type I error
H0 is false	Type II error	Correct decision

The probability of committing a Type-I error is the same as a p-value. α-value can be interpreted as the acceptable probability of making a Type-I error (also called significance level). The hypothesis is an assumption about a population parameter that is subject to a test and rejection based on evidence. A hypothesis test is applicable when the manager has a specific position on a population parameter which needs to be rejected in order to take action. A data scientist typically targets type-I error called the level of significance. If the calculated probability of a given sample is less than the level of significance under the null hypothesis, he rejects his null hypothesis and makes the necessary change.

5.9 CHI-SQUARE TEST

Chi-Square Test of Association: The chi-square test of association helps to determine whether two or more categorical variables are associated. The test has the null hypothesis that the variables are independent and the alternative hypothesis that they are not independent

The test is only suitable if there is sufficient data, which is commonly defined as all table cells having expected counts at least five. For 2-way tables, you can use **chisq. test** (*my table*) to test the independence of the row and column variable. By default, the p-value is calculated from the asymptotic chi-squared distribution of the test statistic.

chisq.test(Health$Treatment,Health$Response)

As the p-value is less than the significance level of 0.05, we can reject the null hypothesis and state that the two are variables associated.

Fisher Exact Test: The Fisher's exact test is used to test for association between two categorical variables that each have two levels. it can be used even when very little data is available. The test has the null hypothesis that the two variables are independent and the alternative hypothesis that they are not independent.

fisher.test(Health$Treatment,Health$Response)

The test results are accompanied by a 95 percent confidence interval for the odds ratio. You can change the size of the interval with the conf.level argument:

fisher.test(Health$Treatment,Health$Response,conf.level=0.99) fisher.test(x) provides an exact test of independence. x is a two-dimensional contingency table in matrix form.

Analyzing Continuous Variables: When we are analyzing continuous variable we may need to answer few questions.

- How to compare means of two populations using paired observations?
- When and how to compare two populations means using independent samples?
- How to test for differences in two population proportions?

Weight reduction program Example: A nutrition expert would like to assess the effect of organized diet programs on the weight of the participants. She randomly chooses 60 participants of the diet program and measures their weight (in kg) just before enrolling in the program and immediately after the completion of the program. Based on this evidence, is the New diet program effective in reducing weight? A health chain can recommend a conventional low-calorie diet for free or can recommend New diet by paying a licensing fee. The firm has determined that it is worth paying the licensing fee if they can gain enough additional members, which is possible if New diet reduces average weight by 3 Kg or more compared to the conventional low-calorie diet. The firm collects weight loss data from two simple random samples of people, one of whom goes through New diet and the other through the conventional diet for 6 months

5.10 T-TEST

One-sample t-test is used to compare the mean value of a sample with a constant value denoted m0. It has the null hypothesis that the population mean is equal to m0, and the the alternative hypothesis that it is not.

```
# One sample t-test
setwd("D:/R data")
WR_Trt <- read.csv("Wt_red.csv")
fix(WR_Trt)
OS_ttest <- WR_Trt[which(WR_Trt$Treatment=="Dummy Pill"),]
OS_ttest$Change <- OS_ttest$Before-OS_ttest$After
fix(OS_ttest)
OS_tt_res<- t.test(OS_ttest$Change, mu=3)
```

The mu argument gives the value with which you want to compare the sample mean. It is optional and has a default value of 0. By default, R performs a two-tailed test. To perform a one-tailed test, set the alternative argument to "greater" or "less". To adjust the size of the interval, use the conf.level argument:

```
t.test(OS_ttest$Change, mu=1, alternative="greater")
```

t.test(OS_ttest$Change, mu=1, conf.level=0.99)

Two-sample t-test is used to compare the mean values of two independent samples, to determine whether they are drawn from populations with equal means. It has the null the hypothesis that the two means are equal, and the alternative hypothesis that they are not equal.

To perform a two-sample t-test with data in stacked form, use the command: t.test(values~groups, dataset), where values are the name of the variable containing the data values and groups is the variable containing the sample names. If the grouping variable has more than two levels, then you must specify which two groups you want to compare.

t.test(WR_Trt$Change~WR_Trt$Treatment, WR_Trt, Treatment %in% c("Old_Trt", "Test_Drug"))

By default, R uses separate variance estimates when performing two-sample and paired t-tests. If you believe the variances for the two groups are equal, you can use the pooled variance estimate. To use the pooled variance estimate, set the var.equal argument to T.

Paired T-test: Paired t-test is used to compare the mean values for two samples, where each value in one sample corresponds to a particular value in the other sample. It has the null hypothesis that the two means are equal, and the alternative hypothesis that they are not equal.

paired t-test

t.test(WR_Trt$Before, WR_Trt$After, paired=T)

It is natural and also feasible to take before and after measurements on the same subjects, in this case, we use Paired test.

Sampling Distributions of Means of the Two Samples: The two sampling distributions of means are normal provided Central Limit Theorem condition is met separately for 1.Independence like Who is in a sample does not influence who else is in that sample and Who is in a sample does not influence who is in the other sample. 2.Size conditions like Number of observation in each sample must exceed 10 times the absolute value of Kurtosis and 10 times the square Skewness within that sample.

Example: Proportion of dieters who lose weight: Suppose an alternate metric to measure the performance of the diet program is the proportion of participants who have lost more than 3 KG. The best way to compare the means of two distributions is using paired observations if it is feasible. The average difference of paired sample observations follows normal distribution according to Central Limit Theorem. When paired observations are not possible, we use independent samples and formulate a hypothesis on the difference between two means. It is important to ensure that subjects are randomly assigned to the two samples to avoid any confounding errors. A similar approach can be used to test the difference in proportions between two.

5.11 ANALYSIS OF VARIANCE (ANOVA)

An analysis of variance allows you to compare the means of three or more independent samples. It is suitable when the values are drawn from a normal distribution and when the variance is approximately the same in each group. The null hypothesis for the test is that the mean for all groups is the same, and the alternative hypothesis is that the mean is different for at least one pair of groups.

Let us think about the following questions and try to answer them with a case study.

- Why is an analysis of variance (ANOVA) required to compare means of populations?
- What is the principal of sum of squares?
- How to conduct the ANOVA test?
- What follow-up analysis should be done if ANOVA test is significant?

Case Study: Weight reduction program: Suppose the nutrition expert would like to do a comparative evaluation of three diet programs. She randomly assigns an equal number of participants to each of these programs from a common pool of volunteers. Suppose the average weight losses in each of the groups (arms) of the experiments are 4 kg, 7 kg, 5.4 kg. What can she conclude? Here, Two kinds of variation matter. Not every individual in each program will respond identically to the diet program. It is Easier to identify variations across programs if variations within programs are smaller, Hence the method is called Analysis of Variance (ANOVA). Formalizing the intuition behind variations. What is more surprising and useful is: Sum of Squares Total (SST), Sum of Squares Treatment (SSTR), Sum of Squares Error (SSE)

Statistical test for equality of means:

- n subjects equally divided into r groups
- Hypotheses:H0: $\mu1 = \mu2 = \mu3 = \ldots = \mu r$. Reject the null hypothesis if p-value < α.

You can perform an analysis of variance with aov function. The command takes the form:

aov(Change~Treatment, WR_Trt)

The results of the analysis consist of many components that R does not automatically display. If you save the results to an object as shown here, you can use further functions to extract the various elements of the output:

aovobject<-aov(Change~Treatment, WR_Trt)

#Once you have saved the results as an object, you can view the ANOVA table with the anova function:

anova(aovobject)

#To view the model coefficients, use the coef function:

coef(aovobject)

#To view confidence intervals for the coefficients, use the confint function:

confint(aovobject)

One Way Anova (Completely Randomized Design)

fit <- aov(Change~Treatment, WR_Trt)

ANOVA Table: If we reject the null hypothesis that all means are equal, the probability of you making a mistake is less than 2.5%. Can we conclude that Test Drug-diet is more effective than Old diet?. The extent of variation between and within groups determines the strength of the evidence against the null hypothesis that means of all groups are equal. The sum of squared deviations totals (around the grand mean) is equal to the sum of squared deviations errors (around respective group means) plus the sum of squared deviations treatment (group means around the grand mean). ANOVA test compares mean squared treatment with mean squared errors. If this ratio is "significantly" greater, we can reject the null hypothesis that the means are equal.

STEP 6

Introduction to Machine Learning

6.1 INTRODUCTION

Have you ever thought that Machines can learn and organize your work more consistently than you did? Did you ever thought about these questions?

- What tasks are machines good at doing that humans are not or vice versa
- What does it mean to Machine learning?
- How is learning related to intelligence? Can a human really create Intelligent Machines which can outperform Human in Many ways? What does it mean to be intelligent?
- Do you believe a machine will ever be built that unveils intelligence?
- What does it mean to be conscious, Can one be intelligent and not conscious or vice versa?

When we see a lot of data we are not sure what to look for and what is in there, and what all is going to be found. Keep this in Mind, learning is not just an attitude to life, but also an attitude to data mining and machine learning, we always approach data and machine learning with this attitude which will take you very far.

Let us discuss the philosophy of learning, we learn in so many ways. We learn by assimilating we read a lot of books, we watch a lot of videos, we listen to songs, this is assimilating. The things we learn need to be applied otherwise we will forget, we apply the things by doing and discussing. This book will contain both theoretical and practical scenarios, we will try to apply some of the things here to actual datasets, you can use whatever the language you want, whatever your favorite tool is (Am using R as a Tool), we apply the things whatever we learned. Once we are done with applying, we can move to adapting whatever you learned and create something new, After completing this book, I want everybody to try these things in solving the business problems.

Let us look at some statement Knowledge is what is left after the facts are forgotten. This book is not about learning specific formulas, but this book is really about the concepts. In this book, I will be covering the topics from different domains, different problems solved by using machine learning. This book will help you to understand what are the different machine learning algorithms we use in the industry to solve business problems.

There are three I's that will make a great product, let us look at radio and TV there were the great products of their times, but today let us see what qualities make a product great. The first I is **Interface** of the product. Do I need to read a manual to operate the product or a 5-year-old or even 70-year-old guy can operate my product, Google search box is the example great interface.

The next I is **Infrastructure,** we are building products not for PC but for the planet. There is a paradigm shift that happened, earlier people build products like windows O/S, Outlook these are all meant for PC. If you look at LinkedIn, YouTube, Google, Facebook these are the products build for the world, they are meant to be used by billions of people across the globe.

The Third I to make a great product is **Intelligence**. If you look at web search on Google and if you type a query it has some auto-suggestion. When you look at them you feel like Google is reading your mind, youtube videos when you watch and when it suggests related videos you feels like the product is intelligent. LinkedIn, Amazon, Netflix when you use them and look at the recommendations we feel like they are very intelligent. This feature is known as Artificial Intelligence without which those products might not have that successful. So, whenever you think of building a new product think in this way, that it should have all the Three I s in it. My book deals with Intelligence part and we always discuss how to create an Intelligent product by using Machine learning.

6.2 WHY MACHINE LEARNING NOW?

Machine learning, Artificial Intelligence, Data Mining, Big data Analytics these are all looks alike and almost deals with the same thing. There may be a slight difference in the approach and overlap between them but all and all you need to understand that these are all same. Machine learning is the traditional term being used and we use the same term.

Let me give a perspective of Machine learning: Let me take the example of web page ranking. That is the process of submitting a query to a search engine, which then finds web pages relevant to the query and which returns them in their order of relevance. To achieve this goal, a search engine needs to 'know' which pages are relevant and which pages match the query. Such knowledge can be gained from the link structure of web pages, their content, the frequency with which users will follow the suggested links in a query. Collaborative filtering is another application of machine learning, that e-commerce store such as Amazon use the information extensively to attract users to purchase additional goods.

Let us look at spam filtering, we are interested in a yes/no answer as to whether an e-mail contains relevant information or not. This is quite user dependent: for a frequent traveler e-mails from an airline informing him about recent discounts might prove valuable information, whereas for many other recipients this might prove more of a nuisance. To combat these problems we want to build a system which is able to learn how to classify new e-mails. Let us look at Cancer diagnosis, it shares a common structure that given histological data of a patient's tissue, we can infer whether a patient is healthy or not. Here even, we are asked to generate a yes/no answer given a set of observations.

we all work for different companies, we seen specific amount of data, if you step back and look at what the world is doing, it is just wonderful that they collected lots of data, if you look at gene sequence, human genome project, people are collected gene sequences of every organism, it is a billion long sequence you need to analyze now you can Imagine how much data it is. Every time you swipe a credit or debit card you create a lot of data, Every time you buy or sell a stock a data point is been generated, whenever you write a book or a legal document, or whenever you send some satellite, these satellites are collecting all kinds of data.

Let me give some sense of Big data, almost 200 million tweets take place every day and there are around 500 million twitter accounts. YouTube users upload 100 hours of video every minute, on the internet 800 new website are created every minute, Facebook processes 100 of terabytes of data every day, there are 30 billion pieces of content shared every month that becomes 30+ petabytes of user data. Google processes 20 petabytes of data a day, this is about crawling the web, indexing the web, etc. Wal-Mart more than 1 million customer transactions every hour, this is the completely new world we live in Excel spreadsheets are not going to be enough, you cannot load the data into your PC, process the data with your PC, and create insights on data it, is not possible. Let us think how did we get here? we did not get here by accident, Lot of things has to happen to get here, This data explosion is enabled by Better sensors, when I say sensor, anything that collects a data point is a sensor, Thermometer is a sensor, GPRS in car is a sensor, even we are sensors, every time we generate data points, when you make a call from your phone, you are creating data, whenever you are swiping a card you are generating data, I want you to Imagine the new world we live in.

After collecting data, when we derive some statistics, we are still able to generate a lot of statistics and reports and histograms, but that is not intelligence. It is brute force calculations, we need to aware of all the things that we are doing. Machine learning experts think about futuristic things, they say a statement like our technology, our machines are part of our humanity. We created them to extend ourselves, that is what unique about human beings. This statement is true for all times, if you look at the bare men, they created tools for hunting, they invented fire, they created wheels, we want to see very far so invented telescope, we wanted to see very small so invented microscope, whatever we create like aeroplanes, cranes, is to extend ourselves. What is the one thing that we have not been extended, what is the thing that we always want to create and still not successful is our brain when I look at a problem, how do I solve it, when we saw an Image, how do we recognize it? Now, our goal is to create a machine that is intelligent, not just a calculator, not just stores lot of data, not just a complex program, but how do I make an Intelligent machine as intelligent as the human brain.

Let us even look at the evolution of computers, Imagine the first computer been created, you need to go inside the computer, connect the wires, that was programming. Then came up with IBM PCs, then laptops, from one computer for the university to one computer every home, thanks to IBM and Microsoft, having a PC at home is their vision.

What is the next evolution of computing? The Cloud computing is the next evolution. This is a data center, motherboards are connected one after another in a rack, we do not need a monitor and keyboard to control them. All the data generated by Amazon, YouTube, LinkedIn, twitter, Facebook etc. sits in the data center. What is the future? The future is what we call as a quantum computer, going beyond the traditional type of computing, which uses the quantum states of the atom, for the computation and to store information. The entire data center can fit into this quantum computer, you can imagine the future of computing. Compare the first computer with the quantum computer, both looks clumsy, but the latter is a trillion times faster than the first computer. In imminent days we can have a miniature of the quantum computers and data centers of the quantum computer think what will happen. You need to remember this like computing power is growing at an enormously exponential rate, and we can deal with whatever the data is and whatever the size is.

Let us look at the evolution of Information technology. I divided them into three parts first one is Indexing Era, where all we have to do was figure out the way to collect the data, store it in a database such a way that we can retrieve it with an SQL query. That was the Indexing Era, this is where even the modern search engines fall into this category, Even Google search is gigantic indexing system, the key is the word and the value is the document that contains all the words, but essentially it is nothing more than an SQL system. People asked for the basic queries like can I take the average of all the people working in a department, or at specific technology with specific years of experience. That is where the indexing system ended. The next era is interpretation era, in this era, we thought like should I able to interpret the data, in a very interesting way, are there any hidden pattern in data, is data saying something which I am not aware of, this is what is unsupervised learning we are going to learn. This is about going beyond querying, and letting the data speak about what it has because I am going ask questions more than a simple query. We see a lot of examples on this throughout the book.

The next era is intelligence era this is where we go into decision making. Can I use my data, not just as a database, can I also make predictions about tomorrow?, Is this customer going to churn?, Who is the person you may recommend next in LinkedIn?, What is the new product that I should create for market?, How can I make decision based on my past experiences, in all the data that I Had?. In intelligence era, the supervised learning and Optimization will fall. There are two goals for machine learning. By now we understand that we are in a data-rich world, and we need to do something to deal with this data. Machine learning is a way to do it.

6.3 HOW MACHINE LEARNING WORKS?

To understand this we need to think about What is the nature of the mind? Do we want to understand how does the mind works? What is intelligence? What is learning? What is thinking? For example, I can build an OCR system to read text characters of a book but does it understands the text. Can we go from reading the text to understanding the text?, Can we go from listening to hearing and understanding the audio?, Can the mobile phone, the video camera you are using to take pictures or videos can understand them and interpret them as the way you do like? How can we extend the machines to this level? That is one of the goals of Artificial Intelligence.

In 1950, Alan Turing came with this test, how can we say that the machines are intelligent, he came up with an interesting test called a Turing test, basically the test is if a person is chatting with two chat boxes, one of the chat box is connected to a computer the other one with real person, the person A goal is to determine which one is machine and which one is machine, if the person A cannot tell he is chatting with a machine or a person then we can say we reached the level of Artificial intelligence. Currently, we talk about our Google search, we are very careful about picking the keywords, keeping the order, since it can only understand keyword-based queries, it cannot understand questions and forget about conversations. We want to evolve from keywords to question answers and even to conversations. The companies like Google is working to crack the issue, and create a machine as good as the human brain.

The second goal of machine learning is derived decisions from data, let me give you some examples,

- In which position the Ad/Page be shown for a given query?.
- Should I approve this home loan or not?
- Which video to show next on YouTube?

All these questions need to be answered by companies, this is not like one big decision, these are all micro decisions, Which need to be taken several times. The goal is to draw the decision more systematically, more organized way.

You should look at your company and see what kind of decisions your companies are taking, is it based on Gut feeling, is it based on previous case studies, or is it really driven from data?. We need to check do we have enough data to make a decision, how do we measure and validate the decision, this is what is the goal of this book to make you a better data scientist, who can collect the data, convert it into a research problem, develop models, deploy the model etc., Data science is a combination of three things: 1. Data 2. ML algorithms 3. Domain Knowledge. All of us might be strong in one or two and we need to pick the others to become a data scientist.

Imagine if you are a computer science graduate you will be happy in dealing with Algorithms, applying algorithms on datasets provided to you by the client, but when you comes to the real world dealing with data is a huge problem. Let us try to understand the word Data Mining, Mining is the process of searching for diamonds in a huge mass of stones. In fact, the data is scrappy, in many ways you can't even Imagine. We need to understand here is the data is not straight forward as we assume. It's Like your 2 year Kid. You like him, but he does lots of things which you are not happy with. He does not behave the way you want. Let us assume that we are strong in both data and machine learning algorithms still we need to know how to apply all these to real world situations because data in different domains behaves differently. Domain knowledge plays a very important role in Data Science. Only when you are strong in domain you will understand which parameter to look for?, What kind of features to look for?. So over the years of experience, I understood that all these three plays a vital role in Data Science. The people who are strong in all these three will be called as Data scientists. Hopefully, after reading this book you will become strong in all the three things.

6.4 TYPES OF MACHINE LEARNING

Unsupervised Learning: You have been given a bunch of data, you not been told what to look for? Now you can be more creative. Just Imagine you provided a Paper, sketch pens, and all the other stuff to your kid and ask him to draw something. He can be very creative and draw whatever he likes and explains to you what the picture it is. This is unsupervised Learning. In this, we try to find the structure and grammar in the data so that we can sense of data. In unsupervised learning what we are working on is Unlabeled data.

Imagine I given you all the YouTube videos, which video is watched for how many times, and who watched which video but did not tell what to do with that then it becomes unsupervised problem.

Supervised Learning: Imagine your kid just comes back to you and asked what to draw? if you give the next input like draw a Tree or draw a House then that becomes supervised learning. That means Supervised learning is when you know what to look for. In supervised learning, we have labeled data and we are trying to find is structure as well as which variable causes the other variable (Structure and Causality) by building Models.

When you are building a model, which says predict Fraud, Predict Customer churn, predict the next youtube video the customer will watch, predict the LinkedIn recommendation, Predict Cancer, when you give a very specific problem then it becomes a Supervised learning.

Let us think about Unsupervised learning, Imagine that you are starting a new business, You gone through different case studies and finds out 20 CRM (Customer Relationship Management) issues, Now we can work on those 20 CRM Issues and may feel happy that you found answers for all the issues. But can you stay comfortable with them? Are we guaranteed that there will not be any other issues? What is the problem with this approach? Let us imagine all the case studies are in western countries, and you want to apply that in India. The issues in India would be very tricky and can be very different.

Just Imagine, Why Amazon could not have worked in India as it is? because in India, Fabmart (many people believes Flipkart) innovated a new concept called cash on delivery (COD), without that option, in India Amazon would not see success. So we have to be humble around your domain knowledge. we need to check if data is saying something to you, that's where we open up and say let me do Unsupervised learning. Let me see what the data is saying beyond what I thought.

Semi-supervised learning: In this type of learning, you been provided with labeled and unlabeled data the amount of labeled data is less compared to the total amount of data. Semi-supervised learning is all about how do you utilize unsupervised learning in combination with the labeled data to build the even better model.

Active Learning: Let us say we have 2000 examples of labeled data, the labeling process is very costly, I have to pick the next guy out of 10 million examples still unlabeled, need to pick the next 20 pictures because I just have constraints like funding and time, which examples should I label first? Because that will determine the next model you will build. This is called active learning.

Reinforcement learning: In this type of learning, we not building a model which maps A to B, but we are building a model which maps the whole sequence of actions into an outcome. Like playing chess, each coin position will determine whether you will win or lose, You cannot evaluate a single step but you can evaluate the whole game as a unit.

Imagine a bank scenario where it evaluates its customers based on the sequence of actions from opening an account to closing the account. Series of actions becomes leads to the customer becomes loyal or churn. Eventually when he churns then you will understand either one or more actions in that sequence were wrong. That means you work over a series of decisions, not a single one.

Let me take an example of Google ad words, you come in, you open a business, you open an ad words account, and specify these are the keywords we want to use for my business, Now lot of fraud happens, what happens, people use words like Mahatma Gandhi for a toy shop, why? the customer applied this trick? you know that's a good query when a good query is there my ad will show up, but it is irrelevant.

Now there are good machine learning algorithms which determine whether the keyword is relevant to the business or not. But sometimes the decisions were very fuzzy. Now machine learning algorithm cannot give you the solution, you need to take the final call because the machine learning model is not able to decide. That's when there is a lot of active learning happens. So we need to understand that there is no pure machine learning driven system, we always combine machine learning with human thinking. we automate the most, but when the machine is not sure about what to do, we use human thinking.

STEP 7

Dimensionality Reduction

7.1 INTRODUCTION

If I have hundreds of variables, it is not that easy to create scatter plots and find out relations between variables. To understand the data what we can do beyond scatter plots? we do dimensionality reduction, in a principled way and one of the most commonly used algorithms called principal component analysis. With a large number of variables, the dispersion matrix may be too large to study and interpret properly. There would be too many pairwise correlations between the variables to consider. Graphical display of data may also not be of particular help in case the data set is very large. To interpret the data in a more meaningful form, it is, therefore, necessary to reduce the number of variables to a few, interpretable linear combinations of the data. Each linear combination will correspond to a principal component. When we face a situation where we have a huge set of features with fewer data points, In this situation fitting a model may result in lower predicting power. This is called Curse of Dimensionality. Here the solution can be either add more data points or decrease the feature space. This is called dimensionality reduction.

7.2 DIFFERENT DIMENSIONALITY REDUCTION TECHNIQUES

When we are dealing with huge data we are not sure about the usefulness of the information collected. So, we tend to delete some variables assuming that those are not really useful. This might not be a correct approach since there are few techniques available to club these variables together and create a new Factor or Principal Component.

There are Many techniques we can use for Dimensionality reduction like

1. Factor Analysis,
2. Principal Component Analysis, 3. Discriminant Analysis. Etc. We are going to study this algorithm now, Let us understand why we do the principal component analysis. Principal component Analysis is one of the method used to understand structure in the data, shape of the data, covariance of the data, which is not possible with simple scatter plots.

Factor analysis is helpful in the following cases:

- When we have a large number of variables in our data set and we need to reduce this number.
- Before performing regression or cluster analysis on a data set with correlated variables.
- When analyzing survey results where responses to many questions tend to be highly correlated.

Prior to performing Dimensionality reduction, we need to check whether dimensionality reduction is required or not, by checking the Multicollinearity. We perform dimensionality reduction when OLS assumptions are violated due to Multicollinearity. In dimensionality reduction, we can take either 1. Feature Extraction approach or 2. Feature selection approach.

7.3 MULTICOLLINEARITY

Multicollinearity means independent variables are highly correlated to each other. In regression analysis, it's an important assumption that regression model should not be faced with a problem of Multicollinearity.

Why is Multicollinearity a problem?: If the purpose of the study is to see how independent variables impact dependent variable, and if these explanatory variables are highly correlated, it's hard to tell which specific variable has an effect on the dependent variable. Another way to look at Multicollinearity problem is : individual t-test P values can be misleading. It means a P value can be high which means the variable is not important, even though the variable is important.

How to Detect Multicollinearity?: Variance Inflation Factor (VIF) - It provides an index that measures how much the variance (the square of the estimates standard deviation) of an estimated regression coefficient is increased because of collinearity.

Interpretation of VIF: If the variance inflation factor of a predictor variable is 5 this means that variance for the coefficient of that predictor variable is 5 times as large as it would be if that predictor variable were uncorrelated with the other predictor variables.

Case Study: Assume that you are analyzing a Product (Washing Machine), you collected information from different users across country by asking the following questions:

Rate it on 1-5 scale (1: Very Low, 5: - Very High)

- How Good looking the Product is?
- How Comfortable you are in using the product?
- How often you faced any difficulties in using the product?
- How often you called the customer care?
- How is the response from the Call center?
- 6: How satisfied you are with our product?

You want to find out whether these variables has Multicollinearity problem or not. We can do that by running lm model and by calculating VIF(Variance Inflation Factor).

#Step 1: Read the data

setwd('D:/R data')

Cus.drt <- read.csv("Cus_satis.csv", header=T)

#Step 2: Find out Multicollinearity issue

Model = lm(Overall ~ ., data=Cus.drt)

Rsq = summary(Model)$r.squared

vif = 1/(1 - Rsq)

vif

Since the obtained vif value is less than 5 we can say that the Multicollinearity problem is not existent.

7.4 PRINCIPAL COMPONENT ANALYSIS

PCA: If we have lesser number of features, we can use scatter plots to evaluate them. But Imagine how will you explore a 100-dimensional data. Can we do pairwise scatter plots even for this? Here still we want to know what is the structure in the data. What is next kind of thing beyond scatter plots? That's what we call Projections, the Principal component Analysis.

Let us discuss what is PCA? and why is very useful? Let us even understand if not PCA then what other techniques can be used?. PCA is a technique used to understand the **Structure** of the data, **Shape** based on covariance of the data.

Let us understand what is a Projection? We use this term projection quite frequently, so let us understand what it is. Let me take few examples to explain this term. Imagine we are on the cricket field, looking at three stumps we use in cricket. This is a 3-dimensional structure. Imagine we taken a torch light, focus the light on the stumps and observe the shadow at the other side. This is called projection. If we change the source of light by different angles, we get different projection. Data is still the same, what we are doing is we are projecting them in a different direction to get different Dimensions. Assume that if we project them horizontally at 180 degrees angle we get a straight line as the projection. Now understand the dimension of a straight line. It is 1- dimensional. But we need to think, what is the information loss when we project the data at 180 degrees angle? If the original data has been removed after the projection can we reconstruct the data? How much information we lost? These are the questions we need to ask ourselves before projecting the data.

PCA is a linear orthogonal transformation that transforms the data to a new coordinate system such that the greatest variance by any projection of the data comes to lie on the first coordinate the second greatest variance on the second coordinate, and so on. PCA uses an orthogonal projection of highly correlated variables to a set of values of linearly uncorrelated variables called principal components. The number of principal components is less than or equal to the number of original variables. This linear transformation is defined in such a way that the first principal component has the largest possible variance. It accounts for as much of the variability in the data as possible by considering highly correlated features.

Now let us understand the terminology:

1.   Direction of projection: The light source and the angle of the light
2.   Raw data in 3d space: the actual stumps, which are fixed in a 3-dimensional space.
3.   Projected data in 2-D space: the shadow at the other end.

Depending on the direction of the projection the shadow will change but not the data. If I change the light further, I get a different projection. So, The projection that we get is the function of where the light is coming from and always the shadow is on the other side. Imagine we projected the three stumps from four different angles and we get A,B,C,D Projections. Now how can we decide which of these projections in A,B,C,D is the best Projection? We measure the goodness of a projection based on how much information it can preserve. The projection that preserves the maximum information is called the best projection. Assume that we consider 'A' as the best projection? what the projection A is doing differently than others? What happens when we do other projections are we lose information. Actually, the raw data is in 3 dimensions, then we did a projection, the projection is an approximation of raw data. after projection, we are getting 2-dimensional space that means we are losing some information because we are going from 3D to 2D.

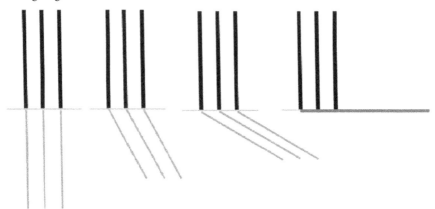

The goal of dimensionality reduction, the projection is to lose the minimum amount of information. So, the correct answer depends on the criteria which we are using. Here our criteria is to minimize the loss of information or the projection that preserves the maximum amount of information in the raw data, is the best projection. In that definition, In Projection A is the Best because it preserves the maximum structure in the raw data. Of course, we are going to lose some structure but the loss kept at a minimum. In the case of D, if they show us only the projection but not raw data, we cannot reconstruct the raw data. That means we cannot have the idea what the raw data is. We would think actually the raw data is a straight line. So we lost huge information in D and very little info is preserved in D. So, remember this, whenever we project data, we are supposed to lose information, but the projection where we have a minimum amount of losing of information is considered as the best projection. So, we can define the notion of the best projection as the projection where we lose the minimum amount of information.

Let us take one more example, let us imagine a spherical data when e project the 2 D data we will get the data been projected in 1 D space. Here we lost some information because the points on the same horizontal line will appear as one point on the screen. so we lost the distinction. because we cannot distinguish the difference between two different data point on the same horizontal line. but we could able to reduce the dimensionality from 2D to 1 D. Let us imagine if we put the light at different other directions, we get different projections, let us assume if we have three projections A,B,C tell me which is the Best Projection? No, we cannot say because all of them are the same. Whenever the data is spherical, That means it is equally distributed and both the feature are completely uncorrelated, that means the features are completely independent of each other, in that case, no matter what you do in terms of projection, you will lose the same amount of information. That's why we are studying Covariance because we want to get to a state, where the data becomes so spherical that all the projections are equally good or equally bad. Conceptually there could be infinite ways to project the data, but when we project data orthogonally, we capture the information of different kinds of data points, and different kinds of structure, in the first case I am capturing the vertical spread and in the other I am capturing the horizontal spread, what I am capturing from one side is completely different from what I am capturing from the other side, and these two projections combined captures the complete information on the raw data.

So, the idea is when I get the first projection where I captured most of the data, what is next best projection which will give me the other info which I lost in first projection. That should be orthogonal to the first projection. Since the data is in 2D I need only 2 projections to capture complete information in the data. Even look at the other two projections the amount of info captured in both the projections are exactly the same. Let me give you another example of orthogonal projections when we use different orthogonal projections which are at 90 degrees angle of each other, the two projections are orthogonal that means the information captured by one projection is completely different from the information captured by other projection, both combined together I will get the complete information. We can say projection is good when the projection takes the shape into account, and preserve the variance. The projection that preserves the maximum variance we call them as First Principal component, the direction in which the maximum variance is preserved. Here, Variance means the amount of Information is preserved.

Imagine if the feature has no variance, then it does not have information content in it. So variance preservation is one of the criteria in best projection. The first principal component captures the maximum variance and whatever the variance remained would be captured by the second Principal component and so on and so forth. Now imagine if you have 100-dimensional data, still the First principal component captures the maximum variance and the second principal component which is orthogonal to the first will capture the second best variance. Then whatever remaining would be captured by the third which is going to be orthogonal to the first two Principal components and so on. In PCA we try to find in a sequential order a set of projections, such that the first Principal component capture the maximum variance and go on and on till the end.

If my data has N dimensions, I can have at most N principal components, Let us Imagine a 2-dimensional data points, there are X data points in the region, Mu is the mean of those data points.(Mu(X)). X(n) is the nth data point in X data points, and if we project them together our concept is to preserve the maximum variance. Let us assume that we projected light from two sources, and Mu(Y) is the projected version of Mean and Y(n) is the projected version of Nth data point.

Imagine, we looked at the projects in both ways, we can understand that the first projection has the maximum variance preserved when compared to the second. Now we should compute what is the projected mean Mu(Y), that is N over all the Y(n). The goal was to maximize the preserve of the variance. I look at the projected space and find out which one is better projection. Projection is nothing but takes the raw data, multiply that with vector, and it gives you a single number, that gives you one projection. Y(n) is the single number that tells me how far is the from the point of that and so on. Now if I want to compute the mean, what I am saying is 1 over N, average over all the Y values. This is only the example of one point, but in reality we project all the points of the space and take the average values, of those points and If I expand the equation W transpose Xn (W is the linear vector, which tells me the direction of the projection,) I take out of the summation, and the remaining part is nothing but the mean.

Mean can be done in two ways like first you project all the data points and take the mean, or take the mean and project all the points later. In both the situations, You will get the same result. Now, what is the variance in the Y space? Variance is nothing but take each data point, How far away is it from the mean, if you have data along with the direction of the cloud, you are trying to preserve or maximize the variance, because the shape you get is longer, that's what we are trying to do, if I substitute the value of Y, Y is nothing but W transpose X here, if I do little bit of math here, what happens is, W transpose covariance times W, this becomes the covariance space. So the Idea is this becomes the covariance, essentially what we are doing is we are taking W transpose times covariance times W and this becomes, into a single number, this number is going to be much lower here, the same number will be much higher in the other case. So, The idea is If you want to maximize the Variance, Find the W that maximizes the Variance.

Now this becomes an optimization problem, this is how we put it, you take the covariance matrix of the data, You have the raw data like four dimensional data, you take the mean of all the columns, we get four numbers, take the covariance matrix, that matrix is called W, you want to find that W, which is the direction, such that the variance is maximized in the projected space. when you do that essentially, you are solving an eigenvector problem, of the covariance. Now you might have understood conceptually what we are trying to do. We are trying to find that direction which maximizes the variance preservation. We find that W which maximizes and that is completely related to the covariance matrix of the data.

Let's look at this in the case of the dataset which has 8 Numeric variables and 500 observations. here you can get the 8*8 matrix, and when we look at the covariance, the diagonal is the variance of each feature, what is the spread of the feature itself, it is an 8*8 matrix. We have taken the summation over the 500 points, each of this is summation of size 8*8, mu of x and mu of x is the 8 dimensional point, center of all the points, Xn is the nth data point, essentially you are taking the average of 500 8*8 matrix, and that gives you the covariance matrix. When you take the Eigenvector, that becomes the first principal component. when you compute the Eigenvalues essentially, this is what it gives you 8 Eigenvectors. Remember the raw data has 8 dimensions, so the projections are also going to be 8. so we got 8 principal components total, and for each principal component, it also gives you the Eigenvalues, which says in which direction how much variance each principal component is having, we can see the first principal component which, is preserving the very large amount of variance.

In PCA what we are trying to do is, we took the entire variance of the data, we are trying to squeeze all the variance on the first principal component of the data, obviously, we cannot get all the variance on the first principal component, but we can try to maximize that. That's what we say after looking at the result, we try to get maximum possible variance in the first principal component, then second and so on. So, the Idea is 8-dimensional data gives you 8 principal components, but the first principal component will have a maximum covariance. If you going to take all the 8 dimensions then we are covering all the variance, But the data has some noise, it is Ok to lose some information, it is important to keep the right amount of information, and right kind of information, therefore we projecting the data on the 2 or 3 principal components.

Let us see some unsupervised Examples:

In PCA, the projection is one kind of structure, it might think that the data has 200 dimensions or 1000 dimensions, those columns came not because the data has those columns, those columns came because somebody decided that it is an important column to have. It is always good to be conservative and has more columns in the beginning because you don't know how you will use it later. The cab company may collect your data like how much time you can wait, what part of the city you belongs to, what time you start to office etc. They don't know how to use them now, but maybe they will use it later. Generally, we collect more columns to be conservative because later we should not say oh! I should have collected that data field even, that is why we call data collection is an art, it is feature thinking art. But when you collect more columns your dataset becomes fatter, now we need to figure out what is the real structure of the data. So PCA is useful there.

Case Study: A Software organization is facing the problem of attrition and they want to find out the reasons for employees leaving their organization. They collected different dimensions and want to compress them into few features so that they can concentrate on those issues. Now our task is to find out whether we can reduce the dimensions or not. We want to find out how many dimensions are sufficient to carry at least 80% of the variance in the data.

Exploratory factor analysis (EFA) is a common technique in the social sciences for explaining the variance between several measured variables as a smaller set of latent variables. EFA is often used to consolidate survey data by revealing the groupings (factors) that underlying individual questions.

7.5   PERFORMING FACTOR ANALYSIS

#Step 1: Read the data

setwd('D:/R data')

Emp.fa <- read.csv("Emp_satis.csv", header=T)

#Step 2: Install and load the package

install.packages("psych")

library(psych)

#Step 3: Explore the data

head(Emp.fa) #show sample data

dim(Emp.fa) #check dimensions

str(Emp.fa) #show structure of the data

fix(Emp.fa)

#Step 4: Data Preparation

fa.req <- subset(Emp.fa, select=-c(Empid,Overall))

#Step 5: Calculate and display the correlation matrix

corMat <- cor(fa.req)

corMat

Step 6: Perform Factor Analysis

Use fa() to conduct an oblique principal-axis exploratory factor analysis and save the solution to an R variable. To derive the factor solution, we will use the fa() function from the psych package, which receives the following primary arguments.

> *Mod.fa <- fa(r = corMat, nfactors = 3, rotate = "varimax",fm="ml")*
>
> Where,
>
> #**r**: the correlation matrix
>
> #**nfactors**: number of factors to be extracted (default = 1)
>
> #**rotate**: one of several matrix rotation methods, such as "varimax" or "oblimin"
>
> #**fm**: one of several factoring methods, such as "pa" (principal axis) or "ml" (maximum likelihood)

Note that several rotation and factoring methods are available when conducting EFA. Rotation methods can be described as orthogonal, which do not allow the resulting factors to be correlated, and oblique, which does allow the resulting factors to be correlated. Factoring methods can be described as common, which are used when the goal is to better describe data, and component, which are used when the goal is to reduce the amount of data.

#Step 7: Display the solution output

Mod.fa

7.6 PERFORMING PRINCIPAL COMPONENT ANALYSIS

#Step 1: Read the data

setwd('D:/R data')

Emp.drt <- read.csv("Emp_satis.csv", header=T)

#Step 2: Explore the data

head(Emp.drt) #show sample data

dim(Emp.drt) #check dimensions

str(Emp.drt) #show structure of the data

fix(Emp.drt)

colnames(Emp.drt)

#Step 3: Data Preparation

Emp.req <- subset(Emp.drt, select=-c(Empid))

#Step 4: Find out Multicollinearity issue

Model = lm(Overall ~ ., data=Emp.req)

Rsq = summary(Model)$r.squared

vif = 1/(1 - Rsq)

vif

    Since the obtained vif value is greater than 5 we can say that the Multicollinearity is present. So, we decided to go for Dimensionality reduction.

#Step 5: Data Preparation

Emp.pro <- subset(Emp.drt, select=-c(Empid,Overall))

#Step 6: Create Principal Components

Emp.pca <- prcomp(Emp.pro,center=TRUE,scale=TRUE)

print(Emp.pca)

#Step 7: Create Scree Plot

plot(Emp.pca, type="lines")

    #The summary method describe the importance of the PCs. The first row describe again the standard deviation associated with each PC. The second row shows the proportion of the variance in the data explained by each component while the third row describe the cumulative proportion of explained variance.

#Step 8: Perform the summary

summary(Emp.pca)

STEP 8

Clustering

8.1 INTRODUCTION

Clustering is the process of organizing objects into groups whose members are similar in some way, it deals with finding a **Structure** in a collection of **Unlabeled Data**. A *cluster* is, therefore, a collection of objects which are "Similar" between them and are "Dissimilar" to the objects belonging to other clusters. Take an example of a Laptop company who is promoting its latest brand of laptop. They want to customize advertisement models, people who live in one part of the city are different to people who lives in some other part of the city. We need to send a different ad to different people. What did we do here? We do clustering intuitively. We can start with one or two messages and we can do that all the way down to individual i.e. personalized advertisement. So clustering is the thing we do when we want to create groups because you cannot create one message for every person it is too costly at one end of the spectra, and you cannot send the same message to all because it is too coarse. Now what will you do, You do something in the middle which is called as clustering?

Now Think about a customer care center of a Cab company, They do want to know what are the CRM issues, they start with some problems, and solutions and go on refining the problem set based on the CRM issues. Think about this, How do they know these issues even before the company started?. They might have taken the issues raised from previous cab companies, then it becomes a classification problem. Then how do you discover new things that are emerging in your market, we do clustering.

Different types of clustering techniques:

1. Exclusive Clustering (Partitional Clustering): K-Means Clustering
2. Overlapping Clustering: Fuzzy C-Means Clustering
3. Hierarchical Clustering: Top-Down (Divisive), Bottom-Up (Agglomerative)
4. Probabilistic Clustering: Mixture of Gaussians
5. Spectral Clustering

8.2 PARTITIONAL CLUSTERING

Partitional Clustering can be Hard or Soft, in Hard clustering Is like you are grouping the data point to one specific cluster features. It's like since it belongs to this cluster it cannot belong to any other cluster. In, Soft Clustering we consider the data point looks like belong to this cluster but it even has the features of the other cluster so partially it belongs to this and partially to other. So, let me apply both strategies to this data point, that is called soft clustering. Initially, when you do clusters you don't know how accurate the cluster centers are, so you don't want to do hard clustering. If your data have too much noise you don't want to do hard clustering, because you are not sure.

Hierarchical: This is not a clustering technique, this is actually a philosophy of looking at the data, always your data has a hierarchy. No matter what is the domain you are in, it can be your gene sequence, finance, insurance, there is always a hierarchy. The world is made of hierarchies. Hierarchy is an integral part of nature, Brain understands hierarchies. Whenever somebody gives you data, the first question to ask is what is the hierarchy in it? your mental model is always here is a hierarchy. How do you find the hierarchy is up to you. What level of hierarchy you will use is up to you. How many level you care in the hierarchy is up to you. Just think about the menu system in a telecom call center if you have this issue, press 1 and if you that issue press 2 and so on.., even after pressing 1 you will get more menu options and so on. Hierarchy is an inbuilt process in the business system, an organization and even in Data.

Unsupervised learning is all about learning the Structure of the data, when we say structure, it really means hierarchy. You may ask me a question like if everything is there in the hierarchy, then why do we need Partitional Clustering? If we want to do the bottom-up approach of clustering we should know the Pair-wise distance between all the pairs, data points from one another. Is it possible for a large number of data points? No, so, if we do Top-down approach we need to do Partitional clustering at every stage of clustering. The Idea here is, let me build 5 clusters first because I cannot have a menu system that goes on till 100. So, I will build the 5 clusters first, then I build the sub-clusters since I know the data follows Hierarchy. That means I am using both the clustering methods in this but my conceptual model is a hierarchy. That means we use Partitional clustering as part of Top-Down clustering. This is what Industry expects from a Data Scientist.

K-Means Clustering depends on:

- You have to know the number of clusters
- Depending on the initialization you met get different cluster
- Depending on the distance function you may get a different cluster.

When I say distance function, there is no such thing as a distance function, you have to create your own distance function, it is like while going to picnic you need to take your picnic table along with you because we are not going to a restaurant. Like the same, you need to bring your own distance function to machine learning part. This is a very important part, the better distance functions you are able to define the better machine learning algorithms you can create. K-means clustering does not care how do you define the Distance function. if everything is a tool, we do not need to do this course with so much stress. what is your role really being a data scientist? That is where our skill will come.

Now think about how will you define, the distance function between two resumes? Seniority is one, skill set is one, companies he worked for, the university which he attended is other and so on. Think about the distance function between one person profile with other person profile, what is the distance between two movies? actors, director, music you can define very complicated distance functions. So, one of the most important roles of data scientist is to define the distance functions. All the creativity comes in these things, nobody will define these things for you, since you know the domain better, you know the data better, and you know the distribution better, it's your job to define these things.

Now the third kind of clustering is called spectral clustering, Lot of times data comes to us is in this form, like a table, where each row is a data point and we have specific features as columns or dimensions. You can use K-means clustering or agglomerative clustering here only when you define the distance between two data points. Therefore, the distance function is important, but often times you get data of different type, which is of similarity between things. We will not get how the data look like, they will only tell us this is similar to that. In that case data look like a graph where each node is a data point, it does not have its features, all we know is distances between data points.

The goal in clustering is intuitively minimizing the distance between the points and its representatives. Imagine the democratic system, since everybody cannot sit in the Parliament, we send our representatives, such that the representative is closest to all the data points. Use that analogy to think about k-means clustering that a mean vector is a representative of the group of people or a group of data points and a good mean vector has to be close to all of those points that it is representing.

- How do we use this analogy to define an Objective function?
- What are the parameters?

There are two types of parameters, 1. Association Parameter which says that how do you assign a cluster to a data point, and 2. How do you update the mean vector?

Let us look at the Formula of Clustering;

$$J(\mathbf{m}, \mathbf{z}) = \sum_{n=1}^{N} \sum_{k=1}^{K} z_{n,k} \Delta\left(\mathbf{x}_n, \mathbf{m}_k\right)$$

In the formula, you can see two Summation symbols one is for Data points and another is for Clusters, this is nothing to do with Number of dimensions. Here I am using the Euclidean distance function.

While doing K-means clustering. We need to understand that we selected a representative for a group when he moves out from our group to another group he becomes a representative for a new cluster and some other guy will become the representative for the left out the group. The Idea is we can have any number of representatives, But I want to do it in an optimal way. Think this as a chicken and egg problem, if we decide the association then we can compute the mean, or decide the mean and compute the association. These are two related problems and we do not know where to start. We can either start by assigning randomly the cluster centers, or we can start by assigning random locations in the data, as cluster means, either of the two is a valid starting point. It is like this: Given the Delta - find the Mean or Given the Mean find the Delta. When these problems are solved, a stage will come where the mean and deltas will not change that is what we call it as a convergence.

Clustering is the iterative algorithm, we start with some mean vector initially, and random initializations, we will discuss more initializations later, then what happens? what are the points that some go to m1 and what are the point that should go to m2? Then the second question, given the mean in iteration p, we want to find the cluster assignment. When I say Iteration, it is starting from the mean, finding the right delta, and then using the delta to find next mean. So this is one equation. Initially, t is 0 that means it is the 0th iteration, and slowly we increase the t.

When we have the data points, we take the points as vectors and compute the distance, assign the data points to the vector, based on the distance. Then update the mean value, and go for the next iteration. The Idea is to start with some means, we used the mean to assign the cluster, and then we take the cluster assignment to compute the mean. Then we iterate again, and again till it converges. This is called the Expectation step. In the maximization step, it says given that these are the assignments, maximize the objective function.

- E-Step: Cluster Centers --> Cluster Assignments
- M- Step: Cluster Assignments --> Cluster Centers.

Just Think about Walking: If we take the one leg, it is E-steep and then we land the leg and take off the other leg that is M-Step. At any given point of walking, you cannot lift both the legs or land both the legs.

Let us answer two more questions:

- How do we pick K?
- How do we Initialize?

How do we optimally assign representatives to data points? while solving this optimization problem, there is no guarantee that there is one good solution. Now Imagine that your goal is to climb the nearest hill, or the goal is to fall the nearest valley. Either you are falling down to find out the lowest point or You are climbing up to find out the nearest hill, If I want to climb the hill I will walk in the direction that gives me a maximum gradient assent, and I will reach one Peak, but if I start at another point I am going to reach the another peak, and most of the machine learning algorithms have this type of problem, In many cases the optimization function is like this, it has many local optima out of which one is the global optima.

What K-Means cluster guarantees id where ever you start, I will guarantee the local optima, that it cannot guarantee is that you will reach global optima. Therefore Initialization plays a very important role in K-Means clustering. Even if you do K-Means clustering for a million times, nobody can guarantee you a global Optimal solution. What we can do in K-Means clustering is try with different initialization points and find the optima and among those local optima you can pick the best one. So, whenever we are performing clustering we need to try to get the initial points to be spread across among all the data points.

Furthest First point Initialization: This is a technique used to deal with the initialization problem. In this method, we pick the mean first and pick the farthest point from the mean, and use that as the first cluster center. Now consider this as a seed, and compute the farthest point from this new seed and consider that point as second cluster center, now I have two cluster centers which have guaranteed me a maximum spread of the data. Now I need the third seed which should be farthest from both the seeds, we need to say the distance from both the seeds should be at maximum, we compute the score of all the points such that the new seed is at the maximum distance from both the points and then we pick the fourth seed which should be at maximum distance from all the three data points.

We are fine when dealing with 4 or 5 clusters but in real time we may need to deal with hundreds of dimensions and millions of observations, then how will you decide the Number of clusters? I can have all my data points in a single cluster or create a cluster for each data point. Here, both the approaches are not useful. The goal here is to find the right number of clusters. There are two ways to think about. It is based on the business problem that we have at hand. If I give three options like do you want to create 2, 5,or 200 clusters? These decisions are based on our business need. If we say that we can handle of 5 types of complaints because we have a limited resource, going for 200 clusters and dealing with all the complaints separately cannot be done by us because it is much costly, let me group those 200 concepts into 5 clusters so that 5 is a reasonable number to have.

We can use a rule of thumb, is a fraction of the square root of the data. The square root of the number of the data points. We can even decide the right number of clusters by machine learning driven decision. There is a correct number of clusters, for every dataset but the question is can we able to find it or not. The right number of clusters is an important issue because beyond which it becomes noise, below which you are not capturing any structure (Signal). We need to think while performing PCA or K-Means clustering, how much noise and how much signal is there in the data.

We can use Gap statistics to find out the right number of clusters, we try with a range of clusters say from 3 to 20 for each cluster you use either Farthest First point sampling algorithm or multiple random initializations whatever you do you will get some statistics. Plot these statistics and compute the gap and it is going to tell you the right number of clusters. We follow this process all the time, Gap cannot be negative because the expected is assuming completely random noise or completely uniform distribution. Assuming the number of data points that are uniformly distributed that is the worst possible structure we can have, so that is what is used to compute the expected, that will always be lower than the observed. so we are hoping that the data will have some structure which is beyond the random distribution of data.

8.3 HIERARCHICAL CLUSTERING

In this type, we have two approaches like 1. Top down (Divisive) 2. Bottom-Up (Agglomerative). In top Down approach we take the entire set as a single cluster and divide them into two clusters, them from both clusters we divide further clusters, and so on. while making clustering at each step we take either the approach of K-means clustering in the case of multivariate data and spherical clustering in the case of text data. If we directly create 4-5 clusters at one go that is called partitioned clustering whereas this approach of dividing them step by step is called Divisive clustering, like first we create two clusters from the root cluster and then further dividing both the clusters into two each. This approach is called top-down hierarchical clustering and we keep going down and down and so on. Now you can ask, if we take K-means approach and Top-Down approach are we guaranteed that we will get the same number of clusters with same entities, at the end? The answer is No. Hierarchy is the natural way in which data occurs, whenever possible we should think hierarchically, we can always use Partitional clustering, in each level, but ultimately we are doing hierarchical clustering.

Let us look at the other type of clustering i.e., agglomerative hierarchical clustering, this is used very much in the following scenario. Imagine when the data points are not very large, that means we do not have too many data points but we want a really good cluster, in that case, people prefer to use agglomerative clustering. Let us take the example of some gene sequences, we group the genes together and they come up with the cluster. Imagine there are some data points, I want to be able to cluster them and organize them, I used Agglomerative clustering. I could have obtained this, either top down method or by using the bottom-up method. So I am not telling you which method I use, The idea is we can organize the data at a leaf node, into a hierarchy.

Let us take the examples of numbers 0-9 and want to find which are the more similar data points, first we take two numbers which looks very similar, there is a very clear notion, that 1 and 7 look similar so I merge them, so, when I merge them I get a cluster which is of size two, and I have n-2 clusters of size 1, I can treat every data point as a cluster, initially when I have not done anything, each data point is a cluster. Whenever do we think about clustering we can think of what is the smallest number of clusters we can have and what is the largest number of clusters we can have? so, the smallest number could be 1 and the largest number could be the number of data points. Agglomerative cluster helps us to build the clusters from n to one by merging the clusters bottom up. You are going to get the spectrum of all possible clusters between 1 and N.

8.4 ASSESSING CLUSTER TENDENCY

Before applying any clustering method on the dataset, a natural question is, Does the dataset contains any inherent clusters?. A big issue, in unsupervised machine learning, is that clustering methods will return clusters even if the data does not contain any clusters. In other words, if you blindly apply a clustering analysis on a dataset, it will divide the data into clusters. Therefore before choosing a clustering approach, we need to decide whether the dataset contains meaningful clusters or not. If yes, then how many clusters are there. This process is defined as the assessing of clustering tendency or the feasibility of the clustering analysis. We can use statistical and visual methods for assessing the clustering tendency. It can be seen that, k-means algorithm and hierarchical clustering impose a classification on the random uniformly distributed dataset even if there are no meaningful clusters present in it. Clustering tendency assessment methods are used to avoid this issue.

Methods for assessing clustering tendency: Clustering tendency assessment determines whether a given dataset contains meaningful clusters. We can two methods for determining the clustering tendency: 1) a statistical (Hopkins statistic) and 2) a visual methods (Visual Assessment of cluster Tendency (VAT) algorithm).

Hopkins statistic: Hopkins statistic is used to assess the clustering tendency of a data set by measuring the probability that a given dataset is generated by a uniform data distribution. In other words, it tests the spatial randomness of the data. A value of H about 0.5 means that are close to each other, and thus the data D is uniformly distributed. The null and the alternative hypotheses are defined as follow. The null hypothesis is dataset D is uniformly distributed (i.e., no meaningful clusters) and the Alternative hypothesis is dataset D is not uniformly distributed (i.e., contains meaningful clusters). If the value of Hopkins statistic is close to zero, then we can reject the null hypothesis and conclude that the dataset D is significantly a clusterable data.

R function for computing Hopkins statistic: The function hopkins() can be used to statistically evaluate clustering tendency in R.

#1. Read csv file to load the data

setwd("D:/R data")

Clus_ds <- read.csv("Clus_sample.csv", header=TRUE)

head(Clus_ds)

str(Clus_ds)

fix(Clus_ds)

#2. Find out clusterability by visual Method: Create a scatter plot

plot(CAD~Neuro,Clus_ds)

Compute Hopkins statistic for the dataset

set.seed(123)

hopkins(Clus_stan, n = nrow(Clus_stan)-1)

    #If the H value is far below the threshold 0.5,it is highly cluster able.

8.5 DETERMINE THE NUMBER OF CLUSTERS

setwd("D:/R data")

Clus_ds <- read.csv("Cluster.csv", header=TRUE)

Clus_req <- Clus_ds[-c(1,8)]

Clus_stan <- scale(Clus_req)

wssplot <- function(Clus_stan, nc=5, seed=1234){

wss <- (nrow(Clus_stan)-1)*sum(apply(Clus_stan,2,var))

for (i in 2:nc){

set.seed(seed)

wss[i] <- sum(kmeans(Clus_stan, centers=i)$withinss)}

plot(1:nc, wss, type="b", xlab="Number of Clusters",

ylab="Within groups sum of squares")}

#The data parameter is the numeric dataset to be analyzed, **nc** is the maximum number of clusters to consider, and seed is a random number seed.

wssplot(Clus_stan)

library(NbClust)

set.seed(1234)

nc <- NbClust(Clus_stan, min.nc=2, max.nc=5, method="kmeans")

table(nc$Best.n[1,])

barplot(table(nc$Best.n[1,]),

xlab="Numer of Clusters", ylab="Criteria",

main="Choose Number of Clusters by 26 Criteria")

8.6 CASE STUDY

A Multi-specialty hospital Chain dealing with Cardiology, Endocrinology, Psychiatry, and Urology specialties want to create some specific strategies to Improve their Business and to utilize their resources optimally. Now your task is to create Clusters and suggest which should be the strategy to be followed in each cluster.

#Step 1: Install and Load required Packages

if(!require(clustertend)) install.packages("clustertend")

library(clustertend)

#Step 2: Load the data

```
setwd("D:/R data")
Clus_ds <- read.csv("Cluster.csv", header=TRUE)
```

#Step 3: Explore the data

```
fix(Clus_ds)
head(Clus_ds)
str(Clus_ds)
```

#Step 4: Remove the categorical Variables like Id and State

```
Clus_req <- Clus_ds[-c(1,8)]
```

#Step 5: Listwise deletion of missing

```
Clus_req <- na.omit(Clus_req)
summary(Clus_req)
str(Clus_req)
```

#Step 6: Perform Normalization

```
Clus_stan <- scale(Clus_req) # standardize variables
head(Clus_stan)
summary(Clus_stan)
```

Step 7: Determine number of clusters

```
library(NbClust)
set.seed(1234)
nc <- NbClust(Clus_stan, min.nc=2, max.nc=5, method="kmeans")
table(nc$Best.n[1,])
barplot(table(nc$Best.n[1,]),
    xlab="Numer of Clusters", ylab="Criteria",
    main="Choose Number of Clusters by 26 Criteria")
```

#Step 8: Calculate distance: Ward Hierarchical Clustering

```
dt <- dist(Clus_stan, method = "euclidean") # distance matrix
fit.hc <- hclust(dt, method="ward.D2")
```

#Step 9: Create cluster dendrogram with complete linkage method

plot(fit.hc) # display dendrogram

#Step 10: Cut tree into 4 clusters

groups <- cutree(fit.hc, k=4)

#Step 11: Create cluster dendrogram with red borders around 4 clusters

rect.hclust(fit.hc, k=4, border="red")

#Step 12: Perform K-Means Cluster Analysis

set.seed(1234)
fit.km <- kmeans(Clus_stan, 4, nstart=25)

#Step 13: Determine the number of Data points in each cluster

fit.km$size

#Step 14: Show the centers

fit.km$centers

#Step 15: Show the clusters

fit.km$cluster

#Step 16: Get cluster means

aggregate(Clus_stan,by=list(fit.km$cluster),FUN=mean)

#Step 17: Append cluster assignment to the original dataset

Clus_Fin <- data.frame(Clus_ds,fit.km$cluster)
fix(Clus_Fin)

#Step 18: Create Cluster Plot

library(cluster)
clusplot(Clus_Fin, fit.km$cluster, color=TRUE, shade=TRUE, labels=4, lines=0)

STEP 9

Market Basket Analysis

9.1 INTRODUCTION

Market Basket Analysis has several names like Pattern Discovery/Pattern Mining/ Association rules/Market Basket Analysis/Itemset Mining. It Provides insights into which products tend to be purchased together and which are most acquiescent to promotion. Association rule learning is a popular Data Mining technique for discovering interesting relations between variables in large databases.

What Is Pattern Discovery?

Patterns: A set of items, subsequences, or substructures that occur frequently together in a data set. Patterns represent intrinsic and important properties of datasets. Pattern discovery is Uncovering patterns from massive data sets. Pattern Discovery is used to find out inherent regularities in a data set and it can act as a foundation for many essential data mining tasks like Association, Correlation, Time series Analysis, Causality analysis, Cluster analysis, Mining sequential and Structural patterns.

What are patterns?: Patterns are set of items that occur frequently together in a data set, which represents important properties of datasets.

We can Use association rules to answer these sort of questions:

- What products were often purchased together?
- What are the subsequent purchases after buying a Specific Product?
- What word sequences likely form phrases in this corpus?
- what are the frequent items this customer purchases?
- What is the average number of items per order?
- What is the most common item found in a one-item order?
- Since he purchased Laptop, when will he purchase a printer?
- Since he purchased iphone6 will he be interested in iphone7?
- Which site he entered, then where he moved, how much time he spent there?
- Which diseases are more common in individuals with this specific gene sequence?

- Customers who have purchased this product, what other products do they tend to purchase?
- What is the average number of orders per customer?
- What is the average number of unique items per order?
- Unusual combinations of insurance claims can be a sign of fraud, How Can I found them?
- Medical patient histories can give indications of likely complications based on certain combinations of treatments, How often these adverse Events are occurring?

The objective of association rules is to discern exciting relationships among the items. Each of the uncovered rules is in the form X → Y, meaning that when item X is observed, item Y is also observed. In this case, the left-hand side (LHS) of the rule is X, and the right-hand side (RHS) of the rule is Y.

Let us take a list of few transactions given in the Transact.txt file from a grocery store adjacent to a fitness Centre.

We may want to answer the following questions:

- What are the two items more likely to be purchased together than any other two items?
- Which product is never purchased with Jam?

Those queries can be answered by observing the data manually. Now the real problem is How do we generate these rules automatically on large data?

9.2 TERMINOLOGY OF PATTERN DISCOVERY

Itemset: Each transaction that contains one or more items. This is also known as an Itemset. The term itemset refers to a collection of items or individual entities that contain some kind of relationship. This could be a set of items purchased together in one transaction, a set of profiles searched in LinkedIn in a single session or a set of hyperlinks clicked on by one user in a particular session.

K-Itemset: An itemset containing k items is called a k-item set. We use curly braces like {item 1,item 2,… item k} to denote a k-item set.

Support: One of the key components of Association rules is support. Given an itemset X, the support of X is the percentage of transactions that contain X.

Absolute support (count) of X: Frequency or the number of occurrences of an itemset X.

Relative support, s: The fraction of transactions that contains X (i.e., the probability that a transaction contains X)

For 1 Itemset: *Support= Frequency(X)/N*

For 2 Itemset: *Support= Frequency(X,Y)/N*

In the given example, If, Bread appeared 4 times in 5 transactions, that means, 4/5 (80%) of all transactions contain itemset {Bread}, then the support of {bread} is 0.8. Similarly, If 60% of all transactions contain itemset {Bread,Milk}, then the support of {Bread,Milk} is 0.6.

An itemset X is frequent if the support of X is no less than a minsup threshold (denoted as σ). A frequent itemset has items that appear together more than the minimum support criterion. If the minimum support is set at 0.5, any itemset can be considered a frequent itemset if the support of a frequent itemset should be greater than or equal to the minimum support. In our example, both {Bread} and {Bread,Milk} are considered frequent itemsets at the minimum support 0.5.

Confidence: Confidence is defined as the measure of assurance or fidelity associated with each discovered rule. Mathematically, confidence is the percent of transactions that contain both X and Y out of all the transactions that contain X.

Confidence, c: The conditional probability that a transaction containing X also contains Y.

Confidence = Frequency(X,Y) / Frequency (X)

For example, if {Bread, Banana, Milk} has a support of 0.20 and {Bread, Banana} also has a support of 0.20, the confidence of rule {Bread,Banana}→{Milk} is 1, which means 100% of the time a customer buys Bread and Banana, is bought Milk as well. The rule is therefore correct for 100% of the transactions containing Bread and Banana. A relationship is exciting when the algorithm identifies the relationship with a measure of confidence greater than or equal to the minimum confidence.

there is a constraint for confidence, as it can identify the interesting rules from all the candidate rules, it considers only the antecedent (X) and the co-occurrence of X and Y; it does not take the consequent of the rule (Y) into concern. So, confidence cannot tell if a rule contains a true implication of the relationship or if the rule is purely coincidental. Sometimes X and Y can be statistically independent yet still receive a high confidence score. The lift can deal with this issue.

Lift: Lift measures how many times more often X and Y occur together than expected if they are statistically independent of each other. Lift is a measure of how X and Y are really related rather than coincidentally happening together.

$$ \text{Lift} = \frac{\text{Support } (X,Y)}{\text{Support}(X) * \text{Support}(Y)} $$

Lift is 1 if X and Y are statistically independent of each other. In contrast, a lift of X → Y greater than 1 indicates that there is some worth to the rule. A larger value of lift suggests a greater effectiveness of the association between X and Y.

Assuming 10 transactions, with {Bread, Butter} appearing in 4 transactions of them, {Bread} appearing in 4, and {Butter} appearing in 5, then Lift (Bread → Butter) = 0.4/(0.4*0.5) = 2.0

If {Butter, Cereal} appearing in 3 transactions of them, {Cereal} appearing in 4, and {Butter} appearing in 5, then Lift (Butter → Cereal) = 0.3/(0.5*0.4) = 1.5. By observing these, we can say that Bread and Butter have a stronger association than Cereal and Butter.

9.3 APRIORI ALGORITHM

The Apriori algorithm takes an iterative approach to reveal the frequent itemset by first determining all the possible 1-itemsets, for example, {Bread}, {Cereal}, {Butter} and identify which among them are frequent. Let us take the minimum support criterion is set at 0.5, the algorithm identifies and retains those itemset that appears in at least 50% of all transactions and rejects the itemset that has a support less than 0.5, this process is called Pruning.

Apriori pruning principle: If there is any itemset which is infrequent, its superset should not even be generated. In next iteration, the identified frequent 1-itemsets are paired into 2-itemsets ({Bread,cereal}, {Bread,Butter}, …) and again evaluated to spot the frequent 2-itemsets among them. This is an iterative process, at each iteration, the algorithm checks whether the support criterion can be met or not. If it met the criterion, the algorithm grows the itemset, repeating the process until it runs out of support or until the itemset arrives at a predefined length.

Apriori Assumptions: Suppose {Bread,Butter} is frequent. Since each occurrence of Bread,Butter includes both Bread and Butter, then both Bread and Butter must also be frequent. So, if a k-itemset is frequent all its subsets (k-1, k-2 itemsets) are also frequent

Steps in Apriori algorithm execution:

- Outline of Apriori (level-wise, candidate generation and test)
- Initially, scan DB once to get frequent 1-itemset
- Repeat
- Generate length-(k+1) candidate itemsets from length-k frequent itemsets
- Test the candidates against DB to find frequent (k+1)-itemsets
- Set k := k +1
- Until no frequent or candidate set can be generated
- Return all the frequent itemsets derived

Advantages of Apriori Algorithm:

- Uses large itemset property.
- Easily parallelized.
- Easy to implement.

Disadvantages of Apriori Algorithm:

Assumes transaction database is memory resident. Requires up to m database scans. *Apriori* algorithm can be very slow and the bottleneck is candidate generation. For example, if the transaction DB has 10^4 frequent 1-itemsets, they will generate 10^7 candidate 2-itemsets even after employing the downward closure. To compute those with sup more than **minsup**, the database needs to be scanned at every level. It needs $(n +1)$ scans, where n is the length of the longest pattern.

Methods to Improve Apriori's Efficiency:

1. Hash-based itemset counting: A k-itemset whose corresponding hashing bucket count is below the threshold cannot be frequent
2. Transaction reduction: A transaction that does not contain any frequent k-itemset is useless in subsequent scans
3. Partitioning: Any itemset that is potentially frequent in DB must be frequent in at least one of the partitions of DB
4. Sampling: mining on a subset of given data, lower support threshold + a method to determine the completeness
5. Dynamic itemset counting: add new candidate itemset only when all of their subsets are estimated to be frequent

There are many applications of Association Rules which includes:

✓   Market basket analysis
✓   Physical or logical placement of product within related categories of products,
✓   Cross-marketing,(Cross Selling, Up selling)
✓   Catalog Design,
✓   Sale campaign analysis,
✓   Promotional programs,
✓   Click stream analysis or Web log analysis,
✓   Biological sequence analysis,
✓   a loyalty card program
✓   recommender systems like Amazon, Facebook, LinkedIn, and Netflix.

9.4 CASE STUDY

Let us take a dataset of transactions near a fitness center at early morning. Let us understand what are the frequent purchases the Joggers or walkers make and find the association between them so that the shopkeeper want to keep the required things ready for his customers.

Step 1: Load the data set

setwd("D:/R data")

basket <-read.table("Transact.txt", header=TRUE, sep="\t")

Step 2: See first 10 observations

head(basket, n=10)

Step 3: Understand The structure and descriptor portion of the data

str(basket)

Step 4: Convert Numeric variables as factors if necessary

fac <- c(1,2,4)

basket[,fac] <- lapply(basket[,fac],factor)

str(basket)

Step 5: Split data

dt <- split(basket$Products, basket$ID)

Step 6: Load the Required packages and libraries

if(!require(arules)) install.packages("arules")

We are now ready to mine some rules. You will always have to pass the minimum required support and confidence. Assume that We would like to set the minimum support to 0.3 and the minimum confidence of 0.8. We want to show the top 5 rules

Step 7: Obtain the Rules

rules <- apriori(basket, parameter = list(supp = 0.3, conf = 0.8))

Step 8: Convert data to transaction level

dt2 = as(dt,"transactions")

summary(dt2)

inspect(dt2)

Step 9: Find the Most Frequent Items

itemFrequency(dt2, type = "relative")

itemFrequencyPlot(dt2,topN = 5)

Step 10: Aggregate and concise the rules:

If rules are excessively long. We can concise rules by adding a *"maxlen"* parameter to your Apriori function:

> *rules = apriori(dt2, parameter=list(support=0.3, confidence=0.8))*
>
> *rules = apriori(dt2, parameter=list(support=0.3, confidence=0.8, minlen = 3))*
>
> *rules = apriori(dt2, parameter=list(support=0.3, confidence=0.8, maxlen = 4))*

Step 11: Convert rules into data frame

rules3 = as(rules, "data.frame")

write(rules, "D:\\rules.csv", sep=",")

Step 12: Show only particular product rules

inspect(subset(rules, subset = rhs %pin% "Bread"))

Step 13: Show the top 10 rules

options(digits=2)

inspect(rules[1:10])

Step 14: Get Summary Information

summary(rules)

Step 15: Sort the rules as we want to write the most relevant rules first by confidence or by lift

rules<-sort(rules, by="confidence", decreasing=TRUE)

rules<-sort(rules, by="lift", decreasing=TRUE)

Step 16: Remove Unnecessary Rules

Sometimes, rules will repeat, As an analyst you can elect to drop the item from the dataset. Alternatively, you can remove redundant rules generated.

> *subset.matrix <- is.subset(rules, rules)*
>
> *subset.matrix[lower.tri(subset.matrix, diag=T)] <- NA*
>
> *redundant <- colSums(subset.matrix, na.rm=T) >= 1*
>
> *which(redundant)*
>
> *rules.pruned <- rules[!redundant]*
>
> *rules<-rules.pruned*

Step 17: Clean Rules

rules3$rules=gsub("\\{", "", rules3$rules)

rules3$rules=gsub("\\}", "", rules3$rules)

rules3$rules=gsub("\"", "", rules3$rules)

Step 18: Split the Rule

library(splitstackshape)

Rules4=cSplit(rules3, "rules","=>")

names(Rules4)[names(Rules4) == 'rules_1'] <- 'LHS'

Rules5=cSplit(Rules4, "LHS",",")

Rules6=subset(Rules5, select= -c(rules_2))

names(Rules6)[names(Rules6) == 'rules_3'] <- 'RHS'

Step 19: Targeting Items:

Now that we know how to generate rules, limit the output, let's say we wanted to target items to generate rules. There are two types of targets we might be interested in that are illustrated with an example of "Bread":

> # What are customers likely to buy before they purchase "Bread"
>
> *rules<-apriori(data=dt, parameter=list(supp=0.5,conf = 0.8),*
>
> > *appearance = list(default="lhs",rhs="Bread"), control = list(verbose=F))*
>
> *rules<-sort(rules, decreasing=TRUE,by="confidence")*
>
> *inspect(rules[1:4])*
>
> # What are customers likely to buy if they purchased "Bread"
>
> *rules<-apriori(data=dt, parameter=list(supp=0.5,conf = 0.7),*
>
> > *appearance = list(default="rhs",lhs="Bread"), control = list(verbose=F))*
>
> *rules<-sort(rules, decreasing=TRUE,by="confidence")*
>
> *inspect(rules[1:3])*

Step 20: Visualization:

Finally we want to map out the rules in a graph. For this we need "arulesViz" package.

> #Install arulesViz package
>
> *library(arulesViz)*
>
> *plot(rules,method="graph",interactive=TRUE,shading=NA)*

STEP 10

Kernel Density Estimation

10.1 INTRODUCTION

When we look at the data the first thing we want to find out is a hat is the structure of the data, for this, we create histograms of the data based on one or more features. Features are also known as Dimensions, Variables, Columns, so we use these terms interchangeably. A histogram reveals many things, like where the data points are more prominent and where is less. We can call it as Probability density Functions since by just looking at the histogram we can say what is the probability that the specific data point occurs. This is one-dimensional Density estimation. But one-dimensional Histogram is not enough, what we really want is joint density estimation.

Do you hear about the story of five blind men touching the Elephant and describing it? What were they doing there? Each blind man in the story explaining one dimension of the elephant and finally we can get conclusion because none of them describes the elephant in full. When we are looking at a single dimension we may a get an impression which might not be correct about the data. If we look at the same data from another dimension I may get totally different Impression. Now the real distribution can be the combination of these two in the joint space. The goal of the Density estimation is to find out the Joint Distribution.

Let me give you one more example to understand the density estimation. Let us take our credit card as an example and we have our normal usage of the credit card for many years. If somebody stole your credit card, he may use the card slightly different because he doesn't know how we use our card and where we use our card more frequently. Now Imagine How a credit card company detects this slightly unusual or slightly abnormal behavior? How do we capture this? What the model is doing?. Let me take one more example, We were given an advertisement on Google for a particular keyword, Normally people may click that add at some rate based on a given day and number of queries and number of times it popped up etc. based on these we get approximately some number of clicks. Let us Imagine I have a competitor, My competitor wants my money to be wasted, What he may do is, he may create a robot by writing a program that keeps on clicking the ad for many times, whenever some query raised on that specific point. Now What do you expect from Google? You expect

Google to find out this abnormal behavior, and from which location the clicks are happening. This is where exactly Kernel Density estimation is useful.

Let me tell you a very important principle of Data. The first thing is Data have Hierarchy. The second thing is data have Structure and Noise. Data will always have Structure and Noise. Our goal in Unsupervised Learning (Kernel density Estimation) is to figure out what part if data has the structure and what part of data has Noise. When we did PCA we kept some Principal components and we discarded some other components because we felt that some components have structure in them and others have Noise. How do we decide how many principal components we need to keep? How do we decide how many clusters we need to create? That is our call and that is the beauty if Data science. Here our goal is to figure out how to complex the model you want so that it captures maximum signal and not noise.

If we decide that there is only one credit card user behavior we fail to capture the structure in credit card behavior, because there are different kinds of people with different kinds of credit card behaviors like how teenagers use the card and how house maker use the card and how a student use the card etc. Based on the domain you are dealing you need to decide the structure and noise ratio and how much data or noise can we expect here? Let me take a simple example for this, if we are dealing with text data, if we look at a bunch of scientific papers we can expect more data and less noise there because those papers are well written and there would not be ay spelling and grammatical mistakes. But if we are dealing with twitter data, we can have many spelling mistakes. Based on these we need to make a call on how much data we need to capture and how complex my model would be. The noise can be natural and noise can be intentional. In credit card scenario the fraud is an intentional noise and in twitter, it is unintentional noise.

10.2 WHAT IS A KERNEL?

A kernel is a special type of probability density function (PDF) with the added property that it must be non-negative, even and real-valued.

What is Kernel Density Estimation?: Kernel density estimation is a non-parametric method of estimating the probability density function (PDF) of a continuous random variable. It is non-parametric because it does not assume any underlying distribution for the variable. The kernel density estimation approach overcomes the discreteness of the histogram approaches by centering a smooth kernel function at each data point then summing to get a density estimate. Essentially, at every data point, a kernel function is created with the data point at its center, this ensures that the kernel is symmetric about the data. The PDF is then estimated as an average of the observed data points to create a smooth approximation, of data to ensure that it satisfies the following properties of a PDF. Every possible value of the PDF i.e. the function is non-negative. The definite integral of the PDF over its support set equals to 1.

Kernel Density Estimate is a sum of bumps, which is assigned to every data point, and the size of the bump represents the probability assigned to the *neighborhood of values* around that data point. Each bump is centered at the data point, and it spreads out symmetrically to cover the data point's neighboring values. Each kernel has a bandwidth, and it determines the width of the bump. A bigger bandwidth results in a shorter and wider bump that spreads out farther from the center and assigns more probability to the neighboring values.

10.3 STEPS IN CONSTRUCTING A KERNEL DENSITY ESTIMATE

1. Choose a kernel, Common ones are like normal (Gaussian), uniform (rectangular).
2. At each data point build the scaled kernel function where K() is your chosen kernel function. The parameter h is called the bandwidth, the window width, or the smoothing parameter.
3. Add all of the individual scaled kernel functions and divides by n, this places a probability of 1/n to each Xi. It also ensures that the kernel density estimate integrates to 1 over its support set.

Choosing the Bandwidth:

Choosing the bandwidth is the most difficult step in creating a good kernel density estimate that captures the underlying distribution of the variable. We can follow simple rules like:

1. A small h results in a small standard deviation, and the kernel places most of the probability on the data points. We Use this when the sample size is large and the data are tightly packed.
2. A large h results in a large standard deviation, and the kernel spreads more of the probability from the data point to its neighboring values. We Use this when the sample size is small and the data are sparse. The density() function in R computes the values of the kernel density estimate. Applying the plot() function to an object created by density() will plot the estimate. Applying the summary() function to the object will reveal useful statistics about the estimate. We use this method to find out the structure and grammar in the data. If we listen to a piece of music, we can say that it is from Rahman or Ilaya raja. How can we do this? our brain has stored music and finds out the structure in specific sequence. By the way, we do a lot of density estimation in our brain.

Let us assume that all the cars in the world are of same color and shape, we saw a lot of data, try to compress it into a model. We cannot remember all the cars but we still can recognize the new car because we saw a lot of data, we recognize how the cars are and then when I see another data or a new object I can say this is a car. What is this going on? what does your brain do? You see a lot of data, your brain created a model, and whenever you saw a new data point, you can understand it is a car. For this your model is enough every time you does not need the data.

We use KDE technique even to find out outliers. As well as to find out how much signal and noise is there, therefore we can define how the complexity of the model. The more complex the model, we start capturing the noise, if the model is too simple, we cannot capture the structure. So, we need to have the right complexity of the model. Density estimation is a that has a lot of psychological things that we do. Let us Imagine a situation you want to give a Unique gift to your wife. How can she feel/measure unique? She takes all the possible gifts and calculates the probability, if the probability is more we call it as normal. If the probability is very rare then we call it as Unique/ Novel.

Kernel density estimation is used in

- ◆   Credit card Fraud
- ◆   Intrusion detection
- ◆   Seller fraud
- ◆   Terrorism behavior

Density estimation is used in solving classification problems even. Imagine we taken gene sequence and finding out whether he is a diabetic or not, imagine the complexity of the model. We may have 1 million diabetic patients gene sequence data and 1 million gene sequences of non-diabetics. Imagine the complexity here. We collected gene sequences of 1 million diabetic patients and 1 million non-diabetic persons and we are trying to find out which part of the gene sequence should I look at and which Part of the gene sequence I need to modify at the birth of the baby so that he cannot develop diabetes in his entire life. If we know how to build a Kernel Density Estimation we can do such a complicated thing. We try to find out those sequences which are more common in diabetics, and how can I modify these sequences at birth so that they can never have diabetes in their rest of life. To do this we try to understand Density estimation then, we can build such a complicated classifier.

Training: We might have seen lots of data, understand different types and sequences of genes compressing that it into shape. Based on this we try to create a model.

Scoring: After creating the model, apply the model to the new data point, like when a new data point is seen we can say that this is a diabetic gene sequence or not. We can even say that what is the probability that he is going to be diabetic.

While a histogram is functionally appropriate to display the wide-ranging tuition data, it can be visually frustrating to examine the distribution since the viewer is forced to mentally Connect the Dots between the bins. In addition, the bins sizes and midpoints selected appear to hide what are three subgroups within the distribution. The graph can be enhanced by adding a kernel density estimate (KDE) since a histogram can be visually frustrating and misleading, especially when bins or midpoints are not appropriately sized or placed.

Kernel density estimates provide a smooth line to follow, however, similar to the "bin sizing" that can distort the data distribution in a histogram. Bandwidth selection is an important part of a kernel density estimate. In most kernel density estimation techniques, the kernels have the same shape and bandwidth. While there are several bandwidth selection methods that automatically choose an appropriate kernel size, the most popular is the Sheather-Jones Plug-In (SJPI) method, which is used as a default in the KDE procedure.

Other bandwidth selection methods:

- Simple Normal Reference (SNR),
- SNR with Inter-quartile range (SNRQ),
- Silverman's Rule of Thumb (SROT) and
- Over smoothed (OS).

Understanding Kernel Density Estimation with a case study: Let us look at the Jewel data, we went to a Jeweler shop we observed ornaments of different metal and Models. dimension/feature/variable/column. Let us look at the Jewel dataset, in the above data, we want to work on two Features/variables/dimensions/columns i.e., Metal and Model. Metal can take three discrete(Nominal) values i.e., Silver, Gold, and Platinum, Model can even take three values Regular, Fancy, Antique. so, we call this as a classification problem. What we are trying to do here is we want to find out P(Fancy, Gold) and so on. if I could do this for all combinations, we can say we built a model. and throw away the data because we created the model, probability of all combinations.

Let us do this:

P(Fancy, Platinum)= Number(Fancy, Platinum)/Total number of Customers =(15/150)=0.10, so we can say density estimation is really about counting and normalization. If we have real values we bin it and do the histograms, then we normalize it.

Let us think of creating a model:

What is the P(Regular, Silver) and What is the P(Antique, Gold)? If I compute all the parameters I am done. Now, does it matter how big the Jewel Store is and How many Customer are there? if we build the model we can use it in a small store or a very big store. If the data is huge it will make my model much more robust. There is no such thing called complexity in the data, we can have complexity in the model but not in data.

Whenever we think of created a model for KDE, we need to ask ourselves few questions:

- How many parameters are here?
- How many free parameters are there?
- Do we have any constraints?

We have 9 (3*3) parameters in this example and the constraint here is that they should add up to one. So, the free parameters are 8 (Number of parameters-Number of constraints) (9-1).

Free Parameter: To understand free parameter let me take the example of tossing a coin. If I want to estimate the Probabilities it is enough for me to know the probability of Head. I do not need to know the probability of tails because we know that P(tail) + P(head) equal to 1. So whenever we have a constraint the number of free parameters reduces. So I can compute P(tail)=1- P(head).

Constraint: If throw the six faced dice: Probability of obtaining 1: 1/6, Probability of obtaining 2: 1/6,...,Probability of obtaining 6: 1/6. That means all the six probabilities should add up to 1. this is the constraint.

Let us understand computing probability: If you are a person, gets worried with all the things happening around you, you are using Joint Probability. (Anxiety) If you are a person, not at all worried about anything happening around you, you are using Approximate Probability. (Depression).

- Joint Probability(Assumes that everything is correlated): M=M1M2...Mn
- Approximate probability (Assumes that everything is Independent): M=M1+M2+...Mn.

In the first case, it is too complex and in the second it is so simple that you cannot even use this in Machine learning. The art of machine learning is finding out the right complexity model. Imagine that somebody is asked you to find out which is the preferred city for elderly people in India and you collected the following Information like Age, Income, Education Level, Traffic, Pollution, Temperature etc. of different cities. Now we need to answer questions like Bangalore is much comfortable when compared to Delhi in terms of pollution? Then what about traffic? Does city preference depend on age or income? Kernel Density Estimation comes handy in these situations.

Let me take another example, In an Interview, Manager wants to pick those who are very good at coding, he gave a task to the people and explained the methodology to follow, He collected the time taken in minutes to achieve that task. After creating the histogram and observing the plot we can understand that if many programmers taking 15-20 minutes to complete the Task. That means that if anybody taking more than 40 minutes (Outlier), We can say that they don't fit for the programmer job.

10.4 CASE STUDY

Let us understand this with a diabetic case study in which few pregnant women been given Glucose orally and the plasma glucose value been collected after an hour to check whether the lady has the problem of Pregnancy-induced diabetes or not?. The mean and the standard deviation of "OGTT" been collected and we have to create Density plots. From this, we see that, in this dataset, diabetes cases are associated with greater levels of "OGTT". This will be made clearer by plots of the estimated density functions. It shows density estimates of p(OGTT | diabetes=1), p(OGTT | diabetes=0), and p(OGTT). The density estimates are kernel density estimates using a Gaussian kernel. That is, a Gaussian density function is placed at each data point, and the sum of the density functions is computed over the range of the data. The kernel function determines the shape of the bumps while the window width h determines their width.

#Step 1: Set working directory and Read the data

setwd('D:/R data')

Diabdata <- read.csv("Diab.csv", header=T)

#Step 2: Create required objects from Diab data

OGTT <- Diabdata[, 'OGTT']

d0 <- Diabdata[, 'Diabetic'] == 'No'

d1 <- Diabdata[, 'Diabetic'] == 'Yes'

#Step 3: Create the density plot

plot(density(OGTT[d0]),bty="n",lwd=2, col='blue', xlim=c(10,250),

xlab="Oral Glucose Tolerance Test(OGTT)", ylab='estimate p(OGTT)',

  main="Distribution of people by OGTT")

lines(density(OGTT[d1]),col="#FFCCCC")

#Step 4: Beautify the Plot:

#Select and add HTML color code which looks transparent to the plot

  polygon(density(OGTT),col="#FFCCCC")

#Add a line for the mean

  abline(v=mean(OGTT))

#Add a wider and dark gray colored dashed line for the median

  abline(v=median(OGTT),lwd=2,lty=3,col="#999999")

STEP 11

Regression

11.1 INTRODUCTION

Regression analysis is a statistical technique used to infer the magnitude and direction of a possible causal relationship between observed pattern and variables assumed to have an Impact on the observed pattern. Regression will tell you whether the relationship exists? It's up to the analyst to decide whether there is a causal relation or not.

- Statistical – it is an inferential statistics. It (regression) is a mathematical approach and the variables that impact the pattern all are random samples from an underlying population.
- Magnitude - Size of impact, Direction - Positive or Negative
- Causal – Cause and Effect relationship - E.g.: Magnitude of rainfall has to impact on crop yield, but crop yield does not Influence rainfall

Case Study: Let's start with a problem, you work for an insurance company, and you want to understand what causes to fatalities on highways in order to help setting premiums appropriately. We start by thinking about what are possible influencers of fatalities. Alcohol, Month, Drivers, Congestion, What else?. There can be many other reasons for fatalities on roads. It is very hard to analyze all possible fatalities in every country In the World- population. Let's say we decide to collect data that is easily available, We were able to obtain a dataset, that contains:

- Fatalities per month
- Whether the day was a weekend or week day?
- Number of licensed drivers
- Number of accidents month wise
- Number of vehicle miles of travel per mile of road (Congestion)
- Drivers under the influence of Alcohol or not

Now, with this data, we want to analyze the relationship between the variables available and fatalities in order to propose ways of setting premiums that take into account factors that potentially impact fatalities. What are possible ways of assessing the relationships? We can use Graphical visualizations or Correlations.

11.2 WHY REGRESSION?

Regression techniques can be applied to this problem to understand the impact of the variables available on deaths. The advantage of using a regression technique is that using a regression technique is that we will be able to assess the impact of each factor taking into account the impact of other factors are also taken simultaneously as well. First, if we believe that several factors have an impact on Deaths, then essentially we are postulating that fatalities are a function of the identified factors:

Mathematically it is represented as follows:- Deaths = f (Drivers, Congestion)

Once we knew that the Multiple factors has an impact on dependent fatalities, then we have to know how the fatalities are impacted by Number of Drivers and congestion. The solution to our problem is Regression. For the moment, let's confine us to the case where we are worrying only about one variable that impacts fatalities in a linear manner. So, we hypothesize that Deaths increase as a number of licensed drivers in a state increase.

Deaths = f (drivers), where f is positive

Simple Linear Regression: The Simple Linear Regression Model is usually denoted by:

$Y = \beta 0 + \beta 1 X + e$ Where $\beta 0 =$ Intercept, $\beta 1 =$ Slope, e = Error. We need to estimate the betas so we can understand the relationship between Y and X.

Dependent Variable: Y: Predicted Variables: The variable whose behavior we hypothesize can be explained or Influenced by other factors.

Independent Variable(s): X(s): Predictor(s) that we hypothesize influence the dependent variable.

Beta Coefficient(s): The estimate of the magnitude of the impact of changes in the predictor(s) on the predicted variable.

Error: (e): The Impact of the unobserved variables on the dependent variable usually calculated as the difference between the predicted value of Y given the estimated regression function and the actual value of Y.

- If B = 0 then Y is a constant so there is no relationship between Y and X, because, whatever be the change in X, Y does not change.
- What happens when intercept= 0?. Regression Line passes through Origin. (X α Y)
- What happens when Slope = 0?. Regression line will be parallel to X-axis(No relationship between the dependent variable and independent variable).

Coming back to the fatalities example, if we assume for the moment that we only have data on number of drivers, and then our regression model would be,

Deaths = $\beta 0 + \beta 1$ * Number of Drivers + e

If we estimate value of β's, we will be able to understand how strong an impact the number of drivers makes on number of fatalities, and look at what can be done to reduce fatalities. There are many ways of estimating the beta coefficients. For now, we will focus on one of the most intuitive: Ordinary Least Squares.

11.3 ORDINARY LEAST SQUARES (OLS) REGRESSION

The Ordinary Least Squares Regression technique estimates coefficients on the variables hypothesized to have an impact on the variable of interest by identifying the line that minimizes the sum of squared differences between points on the estimated line and the actual values of the Independent variable

- ◆ Coefficients: Betas ($\beta 1$ and $\beta 0$)
- ◆ Minimizes: Least (value)
- ◆ Sum of Squared Difference: Square of residuals
- ◆ Estimated line: Regression Line
- ◆ Actual Values: Values in data set

Clearly, we can fit many straight lines that each will cover some of the points. As the straight line cannot hit all the points, one way of choosing the lines is to identify the line that would explain most variation in Y, or in other words, have least error. The ordinary least square regression finds that line by looking at the residuals (or the difference between the points on each line and actual Y) and minimizing the sum of their squares.

Residuals capture the capture the error in the estimated line (difference between line estimated and real-life values). Once the line is estimated then $\beta 0$ is the intercept of that line, and similarly $\beta 1$ is the slope of that line. How do we in reality estimates the "best" line?

We can be sure that given the data, the Ordinary Least square estimate line minimizes errors more than any other line that we choose. Is there any straight line that can hit all points?

OLS Estimates: The Ordinary Least Squares regression finds that line by looking at the residuals (or the difference between the points on each line and actual Y) minimizing the sum of their squares.

Why sum of squares?: To overcome, Positive and Negative Differences

Mathematically, minimize

$$Q = \sum_{i=1}^{N} \left(Y_i - \beta_0 - \beta_i X_i \right)^2$$

Using Differential calculus we will get,

$$\beta_1 = \frac{\sum X_i Y_i - \sum X_i \sum Y_i}{n \sum X_i^2 - \left(\sum X_i \right)^2}$$

$$\beta_0 = \frac{\sum X_i^2 \sum Y_i - \sum X_i \sum X_i Y_i}{n \sum X_i^2 - \left(\sum X_i\right)^2}$$

These estimates are called Ordinary Least square estimates. And the straight line represented by $Y = \beta 0 + \beta 1X$ will be a here least square line. These estimates are called the Ordinary Least Squares estimate line minimizes errors more than any other line that we choose. Once we estimate the coefficients, we then have an equation like this,

Deaths = Intercept estimate + Beta Coeff * Number of Drivers.

Remember, this is the best-fitted line, but this line will not cover every single point on the scatter plot. If we calculate the values of Fatalities using the actual values of Number of Drivers that we see in the data, we are computing the "Predicted" Deaths. The difference between the predicted value of fatalities and the actual value of fatalities in the data for each value of a number of drivers is the residuals. Using the fatalities dataset, run a simple regression and find out intercept (A) and Slope (B).

Therefore now, estimated regression line will be, Deaths = A + B * Number of drivers

Beta Coefficient: For every unit increase in Number of Drivers, we expect to see an increase in fatalities by given number. That means, for an increase in 100 no of drivers, we expect to see an increase in fatalities by this number. The positive sign on the coefficient on a number of drivers implies a positive relationship between Number of Drivers and Fatalities.

- P-value: H0 – There is no impact of no. of drivers (X-axis) on fatalities (Y-axis)
- P-value: If the p-value is < 0.05 then coefficient is significant at the 5% level.

Lower the p-value the more likely to reject the H0 hypothesis. If P-value is very much less than 0.05, we reject H0. Finally, we can conclude that no of drivers has statistically significant impact on fatalities.

While the regression equation is the best straight line equation possible, how do we assess the effectiveness of the overall model? One way is to look at a measure of "Explainability", that is, how much of the dependent variable Y is explained by X? Or, a better way to put it is, how much of the variance in Y explained by X?

The mathematical way to calculate this is:

$$R^2 \equiv 1 - \frac{SS_{err}}{SS_{tot}}$$

Where, $SS_{err} = \Sigma_i \left(y_i - f_i\right)^2$

$$SS_{tot} = \sum_i \left(y_i - \tilde{y}\right)^2$$

Calculate the R-Square value for example if R2 = 0.9399, it means 93.99% of the variation in fatality variable is explained by the variation in the no of drivers variable. Higher the R2, higher the variation in Dependent variable (Y) is explained by the variation in the Independent variable (X).

Build the model, with the best possible R2 with the data that you have by trying the different combinations of the variables that you have. R2 is the one way of validating the model, but not the only way of validating the model. R2 also increases with the addition of variables, whether relevant or not, so it's better to use adjusted R2measure.

Adjusted R^2: Adjusted R^2 looking at the impact of significant variables in a model. Even if you have insignificant variables in the model, R^2 will go up, but adjusted R^2 will go up only the model contains significant variables.

11.4 MULTIPLE LINER REGRESSION

Now, let's move on to a case where we expect multiple variables to have an impact on a particular dependent variable. This is clearly the case in real life. As long as we expect a linear relationship between each independent variable and the dependent variable, we can use the Least Squares technique to come up with estimators of the beta coefficients. We would again estimate the line across multiple dimensions that would minimize the sum of squared residuals.

Let's think about the three variables that will influence the Deaths are Congest, Drivers, and Alcohol.

◆   Congest: how crowded the City roads are?

◆   Drivers: No of licensed drivers in the City.

◆   Alcohol: 0 indicate driver did not take alcohol and 1 indicates driver did take alcohol

The equation for the OLS estimation would be:

Deaths = β0 + β1 * Congest + β2 * Drivers + β3 * Alcohol + e

Now, we need to estimate 4 Beta coefficients: β0, β1, β2andβ3. We would use the same OLS approach of the minimizing sum of squared residuals across multiple dimensions.

The coefficient of the driver will change because of the now we are also controlling the impact of the congest and Alcohol. If the objective is to predict the impact of drivers, then we do not include the congest variable into the model. In this case, we can drop the congest variable and re-run the model with only significant variables.

11.5 BUILD THE MODEL AND VALIDATE IT ON THE GIVEN FATALITIES FILE

Step 1: Install and Load Required Packages:

library(ggplot2)
library(caret)
library(lattice)

Step 2: Load the data

Fataldata =read.csv(file="D:\\R data\\Fatalities.csv", header=TRUE, sep=",")

Step 3: Explore the data

str(Fataldata)
fix(Fataldata)

Step 4: Prepare the data

4.1 Converting categorical variables to factor

> *Fataldata$Weekend = as.factor(Fataldata$Weekend)*
>
> *Fataldata$Alcohol = as.factor(Fataldata$Alcohol)*
>
> *Fataldata$Month = as.factor(Fataldata$Month)*

4.2 Drop the dependent variable

> *Fataldata_a = subset(Fataldata, select = -c(Deaths))*

4.3 Identify numeric variables

> *numericdata <- Fataldata_a[sapply(Fataldata_a, is.numeric)]*

4.4 Calculate Correlation

> *descrCor <- cor(numericdata)*
>
> *highlyCorrelated <- findCorrelation(descrCor, cutoff=0.4)*

4.5 Identify Variable Names of Highly Correlated Variables

> *highlyCorCol <- colnames(numericdata)[highlyCorrelated]*

4.6 Print highly correlated attributes

> *highlyCorCol*

4.7 Remove highly correlated variables and create a new dataset

> *dat3 <- Fataldata[, -which(colnames(Fataldata) %in% highlyCorCol)]*
>
> *dim(dat3)*
>
> *str(dat3)*

Step 5: Build Linear Regression Model

fit0 = lm(Deaths ~ Drivers, data=Fataldata)

fit2 = lm(Deaths ~ Weekend, data=Fataldata)

fit3 =lm(Deaths ~ Weekend+Drivers, data=Fataldata)

fit =lm(Deaths ~ ., data=Fataldata)

Step 6: Check Model Performance

summary(fit)

summary(fit0)

6.1 Extracting Coefficients

summary(fit)$coeff

6.2 Extracting Rsquared value

summary(fit)$r.squared

6.3 Extracting Adj. Rsquared value

summary(fit)$adj.r.squared

6.4 Stepwise Selection based on AIC

library(MASS)

step <- stepAIC(fit, direction="both")

summary(step)

6.5 Backward Selection based on AIC

step <- stepAIC(fit, direction="backward")

summary(step)

6.6 Forward Selection based on AIC

step <- stepAIC(fit, direction="forward")

summary(step)

6.7 Stepwise Selection with BIC

n = dim(dat3)

stepBIC = stepAIC(fit,k=log(n))

summary(stepBIC)

Step 7: Model Diagnostics

We need to inspect the validity of the main assumptions of the linear regression model. This refers, to the distribution of the model's errors terms i.e., homogeneous variance, normality, and independence. Analysis of observed residuals may help to evaluate the plausibility of these assumptions. Checking for unusual and influential observations is another part of regression diagnostics.

7.1 Checking for Outliers: The car package contains a Bonferroni outlier test which just calculates and assess Outliers.

library(car)

outlierTest(stepBIC) # Outliers - Bonferonni test

7.2 Check the Normality: Histograms and box plots are also suitable for checking normality, along with descriptive statistics like skewness and kurtosis, for example.

hist(residuals(fit))

boxplot(residuals(fit))

 # Normality of Residuals:# qq plot for studentized residuals

qqPlot(fit, main="QQ Plot")

Shapiro-Wilks normality test: #Normality Of Residuals (Should be > 0.05). The null hypothesis is that the residuals have a normal distribution. The p-value of the test statistic is large in this example. It thus follows that the null hypothesis is not rejected.

res=residuals(stepBIC,type="pearson")

shapiro.test(res)

7.3 Autocorrelation: Durbin–Watson statistic is a test statistic used to detect the presence of autocorrelation (a relationship between values separated from each other by a given time lag) in the residuals (prediction errors) from a regression analysis. The p value indicates that there is no evidence of correlated errors, but the results should be viewed with skepticism because of the omission of the missing values.

 # Test for Autocorrelated Errors

durbinWatsonTest(stepBIC)

7.4 Multicollinearity: We check VIF of all the variables to Test Multicollinearity. Variance inflation factors (VIF) measure how much the variance of the estimated regression coefficients are inflated as compared to when the predictor variables are not linearly related. VIF is useful to describe how much Multicollinearity (correlation between predictors) exists in a regression analysis. Multicollinearity is problematic because it can increase the variance of the regression coefficients, making them unstable and difficult to interpret.

We can use the following guidelines to interpret the VIF: If VIF is less than or equal to 1 we can say that the predictors are not correlated, If VIF is between 1 to 5 predictors are moderately correlated and if VIF is greater than 5 we can conclude that the predictors are highly correlated.

 # Evaluate Multicollinearity

vif(stepBIC) # variance inflation factors

7.5 **Ho**moscedasticity (Constant variance): The important assumption of linear regression is that there should be no heteroscedasticity of residuals. It means that the variance of residuals should not increase with fitted values of the response variable. It is routine to check for heterocedasticity of residuals after building the linear regression model. Because we want to check if the model thus built is unable to explain some pattern in the response variable (Y), that eventually shows up in the residuals. This would result in an inefficient regression model that could yield strange predictions later on when we actually using the model.

There are a couple of tests we can use to check the presence or absence of heteroscedasticity 1. The Breush-Pagan test and 2. The NCV test.

Breush Pagan Test

HS_test1 <- bptest(fit) #Breusch-Pagan test

NCV Test

HS_test2 <- ncvTest(fit) #Non-constant Variance Score Test

Both HS_test1 and HS_test2 have a p-value less than a significance level of 0.05, therefore we can reject the null hypothesis that the variance of the residuals is constant and infer that heteroscedasticity is indeed present. We can rectify this issue by using two methods: 1.Rebuild the model with new predictors. 2. Perform Variable transformation such as Box-Cox transformation.

7.6 **Box-Cox** transformation: Box-cox transformation is a mathematical transformation of the variable to make it approximate to a normal distribution. Performing a box-cox transformation of the Y variable often solves the issue of Heteroscedasticity.

Death_Boxcox <- caret::BoxCoxTrans(Fataldata$Deaths)

print(Death_Boxcox)

The model for creating the box-cox transformed variable is ready. Let's now apply it on Fataldata$Deaths and append it to a new data frame. Append the transformed variable to Fataldata.

Fataldata <- cbind(Fataldata, Deaths_new=predict(Death_Boxcox, Fataldata$Deaths))

The transformed data for our new regression model is ready. Let's build the model and check for heteroscedasticity.

Fatal_bc <- lm(Deaths_new ~ ., data=Fataldata)

Perform the Breusch-Pagan test once again to check whether the heteroscedasticity problem is been addressed or not.

bptest(Fatal_bc)

Since the obtained P-Value is greater than 0.05 we can say that the residuals are now Homoscedastic.

7.7 **Influential Observations:** Influential observation is an observation for a statistical calculation whose deletion from the dataset would noticeably change the result of the calculation. An influential observation is defined as an observation that changes the slope of the line. Thus, influential points have a large influence on the fit of the model. So we need to check the influential observations in our dataset. Cook's distance measure is a combination of a residual effect and leverage. the purpose of Cook's distance measure is detection of influential observations and detection of the joint influence of outliers, both in the response variable Y and the explanatory variables X.

#Cook's D plot: identify D values > 5/(n-k-1)

cutoff <- 5/((nrow(Fataldata)-length(fit$coefficients)-2))

plot(fit, which=5, cook.levels=cutoff)

#Relative Importance

library(relaimpo)

calc.relimp(stepBIC)

#See Predicted Value

pred = predict(stepBIC,Fataldata)

#See Actual vs. Predicted Value

finaldata = cbind(Fataldata,pred)

print(head(subset(finaldata, select = c(Deaths,pred))))

Step 8: Calculating RMSE

rmse <- sqrt(mean((Fataldata$Deaths - pred)^2))

print(rmse)

#Calculating Rsquared manually

y = Fataldata[,c("Deaths")]

R.squared = 1 - sum((y-pred)^2)/sum((y-mean(y))^2)

print(R.squared)

#Calculating Adj. Rsquared manually

n = dim(Fataldata)[1]

p = dim(summary(stepBIC)$coeff)[1] - 1

*adj.r.squared = 1 - (1 - R.squared) * ((n - 1)/(n-p-1))*

print(adj.r.squared)

STEP 12

Logistic Regression

12.1 INTRODUCTION

Many research problems have dichotomous outcome, whether a customer will churn or not, whether a loan would be paid or defaulted, whether a patient has cancer or not, and so on. usually, these questions were addressed by either ordinary least squares (OLS) regression or linear Discriminant function analysis. But these are found to be less than ideal for handling dichotomous outcomes due to their strict statistical assumptions, like linearity, normality, and continuity for OLS regression and multivariate normality with equal variances and covariance for Discriminant analysis. Logistic regression extends the ideas of linear regression to the situation where the dependent variable Y, is categorical. We can think of a categorical variable as dividing the observations into classes. For example, if Y denotes whether a particular customer is likely to purchases a product (1) or not likely to purchase (0) we have a categorical variable with 2 categories or classes (0 and 1). Linear regression hypothesis can be much larger than 1 or much smaller than zero and hence inception becomes difficult.

In logistic regression, we take two steps:1.Find the estimates of the probabilities of belonging to each class. Case when Y = 0 or 1, the probability of belonging to class 1, P(Y=1) and 2.Use a cut-off value on these probabilities in order to classify each case in one of the classes. For example in binary case, a cut-off of 0.5 means that the cases with an estimated probability of P(Y=1) > 0.5 are classified as belonging to class 1, whereas cases with P(Y=0) < 0.5 are classified as belonging to class 0. The cut-off need not be set at 0.5. When the event in the question is a low-probability event, a higher than average cut-off value, although below 0.5 may be sufficient to classify. Deciding a cut-off value is an 'Art' rather than science.

Logistic regression analysis used for prediction of categorical (Binomial, Ordinal) variables using a mix of continuous and discrete predictors. Logistic Regression is used when Dependent variable: Categorical and the Independent variables are either Continuous or Categorical. Logistic Regression is used when the research objective is focused on whether or not an event occurred, rather than when it occurred i.e. time course information is not used. Here, Instead of building a predictive model for "Y (Response)" directly, the approach models Log Odds (Y); hence the name Logistic or Logit.

Examples:

- Default - Credit Card
- Response - Direct Mailer
- Acquisition – Customer
- Recommend - Purchase

Multiple Types of Logistic Regression

Binary Logit:

- Used when the response variable is binary or dichotomous
- It has only 2 outcomes e.g. Good v/s Bad, Yes v/s No

Multinomial Logit:

- Used when the response variable has more than 2 outcomes, and
- The outcomes cannot be ordered in any manner e.g. Choice of drink, choice of tourism spot.

Ordered Logit:

- Used when the response variable has more than 2 outcomes, and
- The outcomes can be ordered in a meaningful way e.g. High / Medium / Low, Strongly Agree / Agree / Disagree / Strongly Disagree

Case Study: Let us consider a sample of customers who were sanctioned a Housing loan by a bank. We want to create a model that assesses the effects of multiple factors on the eligibility of Housing loan.

We have the following data available:

- Id
- Age of the Applicant
- Gender
- Experience in Years
- Monthly Income in Thousands
- Family Size
- Education Level
- Loan_Sanctioned or not

One way to assess impact of factors on eligibility of a personal loan is Build a regression model

- Loan Eligibility = f (Income, Age, Education)

What would be the OLS equation for such a regression model?

Eligibility $(Y) = \beta 0 + \beta 1 * \text{Income} + \beta 2 * \text{Age} + \beta 3 * \text{Education} + e$

12.2 WHY LOGISTIC REGRESSION?

✓ The probability of Loan_Sanction is not linear

✓ We see that almost no-one is sanctioned a loan at the low end, and Almost everyone is sanctioned a loan at the high end of Income

✓ The change in the probability of being sanctioned a loan at the low and a high end of Income is minimal, whereas, in the middle of the range, change in probability is large.

What can be the values of Y? If we use a linear regression model, the predicted values are unbounded (-∞ to +∞).But here, in this case, the probability values are restricted to 0 to 1. One way to solve this problem is to take an odds ratio (p/1-p) and then take the log.

- ◆ p/(l-p) - can take values of 0 to ∞,
- ◆ log (p/1-p) can take values of -∞ to + ∞
- ◆ The mathematical concept that underlies logistic regression is the logit, the natural logarithm of an odds ratio.

What is an "Odds Ratio"?: It is a standard statistical term that denotes probability of success to the probability of failure. If probability of success is 0.75, then odds ratio = (0.75/0.25) = 3. In other words, there is a 3:1 chance of success. The transformation from probability to odds is a monotonic transformation, meaning the odds increase as the probability increases or vice versa. Probability ranges from 0 and 1. Odds range from 0 and positive infinity.

The transformation from odds to the log of odds is the log transformation. Again this is a monotonic transformation. That is to say, the greater the odds, the greater the log of odds and vice versa.

Why do we take all the trouble doing the transformation from probability to log odds? One reason is that it is usually difficult to model a variable which has restricted range, such as probability. This transformation is an attempt to get around the restricted range problem. It maps probability ranging between 0 and 1 to log odds ranging from negative infinity to positive infinity. Another reason is that among all of the infinitely many choices of transformation, the log of odds is one of the easiest to understand and interpret. This transformation is called logit transformation.

Logistic Regression Model Form

The Model Form therefore is:

- ◆ Additive: log (p/1-p) = Y= β0+ β1 *Income
- ◆ Multiplicative terms: (p/1-p) = e β0 * e β1 * Income
- ◆ Values of Y are not restricted to 0 and 1.
- ◆ Log transformation has a linear relationship with predictors (a unit change in X will lead to a fixed % change in logY)

- In terms of Y: a unit change in X will lead to a multiplicative eβ change in Y (odds multiplier)
- %change in Y approx. =100 * (e β -1) (for small values of coefficient)

If we wanted the model in terms of p:

$$P = \frac{e^{\left(\beta_0 + \beta_1 X_1 + \beta_2 X_2 + \dots \beta_k X_k\right)}}{1 - e^{\left(\beta_0 + \beta_1 X_1 + \beta_2 X_2 + \dots \beta_k X_k\right)}}$$

Where:

P - Probability of event

β_0- intercept parameter (value of the dependent variable, when the independent variable (x) is equal to zero)

X - Set of independent variables (predictors)

β_k is the slope parameter (change independent variable for a unit change in predictor variables).

12.3 HOUSING LOAN DATA SET

A Bank wanted to understand factors that impact eligibility for a Housing loan, based on historical data of its existing customers.

Data Preparation: Data Preparation for Logistic Regression includes:

- Response Variable coding: The response variable (or target variable) will need to be converted to a 1/0. Code "Sanctioned Housing loan" as "1" and "Rejected Housing loan" as "0".
- Missing value treatment - using logical rules.
- Outlier detection - to ensure we don't have highly skewed values.
- Multicollinearity- two independent variables do not provide similar information.
- Variable transformations- we have a meaningful transformation of variables depending on the research and modeling scope.
- Descriptive statistics - Basic measures of central tendency need to be output to validate if correct data is being used for modeling

Data Partitioning: Divide the sample into 2 sub-samples,1. Development sample (Training), 2.Validation sample. Development sample is the Sample used to build a Logistic regression model. Validation sample is used to Estimate obtained from the development sample will be tested here for comparison and checking the robustness of the model.

Balanced Samples: Ideally: Proportion of 1's to 0's should not be less than 2%. If "rare events proportion of 1's:< 2% - oversample. Keep rare events in the sample as is, and reduce non-events. This artificial approach does not alter the inherent model form.

It has an impact on the constant term or the intercept and has to be corrected once the model is finalized.

Balanced Sample Correction Factor: In this case, we have Logistic regression model form as

Log(pi/1-pi) = a + b1X1+ b2X2 + b3X3.

Logistic Regression Parameter Estimation

Estimation for Logistic: The coefficients for the Logistic equation are estimated using a technique known as Maximum Likelihood Estimation (MLE). MLE is a popular method of estimation as It does not have any underlying assumptions of distribution. When the underlying distribution of error terms is normal, MLE estimates are similar to OLS estimates. OLS like many other distributions is a special case of MLE.

12.4 PERFORMANCE OF LOGISTIC REGRESSION MODEL

To evaluate the performance of a logistic regression model, we must consider few metrics.

1. **Likelihood Ratio Test:** A model created by logistic regression is considered a better fit to the data if it demonstrates good fit with fewer predictors. In likelihood ratio test, we compares the likelihood of the data under the full model against the a model with fewer predictors. Removing predictor variables from a model will almost always make the model fit less well, but it is necessary to test whether the observed difference in model fit is statistically significant.

    We consider Null Hypothesis (H0) holds that the reduced model is true, a p-value for the overall model fit statistic that is less than 0.05 we reject the null hypothesis. The likelihood ratio test can be performed in R using the lrtest() function from the lmtest package or using the ANOVA() function in the base.

    model<- glm(Loan_sanctioned~ Age+Experience+Income+Family,

    data=loan_train, family = binomial)

    model2<- glm(Loan_sanctioned~ Income+Family,

    data=loan_train, family = binomial)

    anova(model, model2, test ="Chisq")

    library(lmtest)

    lrtest(model, model2)

    We obtained Value much greater than 0.05, So, we fail to reject the null hypothesis, and concludes that removing Age and Experience from the model does not have any impact on the model performance.

2. **Variable Importance:** We use the varImp function in the caret package to assess the relative importance of individual predictors in the model, we can also look at the absolute value of the t-statistic for each model parameter.

   library(caret)

   varImp(model)

   varImp(model2)

   By looking at the values we can say that Income and Family size play an Important role in predicting whether the Loan will be sanctioned or not. So we can remove both Age and Experience from the model.

3. **Validation of Predicted Values (Classification Rate):** This involves using the model estimates to predict values on the training set and compare the predicted target variable versus the observed values for each observation.

   Confusion Matrix: Confusion Matrix is a table that is often used to describe the performance of a classification model on a set of test data for which the true values are known.

Confusion Matrix		Target			
		Positive	Negative		
Model	Positive	a	b	Positive Predictive Value	a/(a+b)
	Negative	c	d	Negative Predictive Value	d/(c+d)
		Sensitivity	Specificity	Accuracy = (a+d)/(a+b+c+d)	
		a/(a+c)	d/(b+d)		

   Accuracy: The proportion of the total number of predictions that were correct.

   $$Accuracy = (A+D)/ (A+B+C+D)$$

   Positive Predictive Value or Precision: The proportion of positive cases that were correctly identified.

   $$Precision = A/(A+B)$$

   Negative Predictive Value: The proportion of negative cases that were correctly identified.

   $$NPV = D/(C+D)$$

   Sensitivity or Recall or True Positive rate: the proportion of actual positive cases which are correctly identified.

   $$TPR = A/(A+C)$$

   Specificity or True Negative Rate: the proportion of actual negative cases which are correctly identified.

   $$TNR = D/(B+D)$$

4. **Receiver operating characteristic Curve (ROC Curve):** The receiving operating characteristic is a measure of classifier performance. Using the proportion of positive data points that are correctly considered as positive and the proportion of negative data points that are mistakenly considered

as positive, we generate a graphic that shows the tradeoff between the rate at which you can correctly predict something with the rate of incorrectly predicting something. Ultimately, we're concerned about the area under the ROC curve, or AUROC. That metric ranges from 0.50 to 1.00, and values above 0.80 indicate that the model does a good job in discriminating between the two categories which comprise our target variable.

\# Compute AUC for predicting Loan_sanctioned with the variable Income

library(ROCR)

pred <- prediction(predict, train_data$Loan_sanctioned)

perf <- performance(pred, 'tpr','fpr')

plot(perf, colorize = TRUE, text.adj = c(-0.2,1.7))plot(f1, col="red")

auc <- performance(pred, measure = "auc")

auc <- auc@y.values[[1]]

auc

We obtained auc (Area Under Curve) value which is greater than 90% so we can conclude that our model is working very well and our model is validated. ROC curve is virtually independent of the response rate. This is because it has the two axes impending out from columnar calculations of the confusion matrix. The numerator and denominator of both x and y-axis will change on similar scale in case of response rate shift. This is the advantage of using ROC curve.

5. **Root Mean Squared Error (RMSE):** RMSE is the most popular evaluation metric used in regression problems. It follows an assumption that error is unbiased and follow a normal distribution. The 'squared' nature of this metric helps to deliver more robust results which prevent canceling the positive and negative error values. It avoids the use of absolute error values which is highly undesirable in mathematical calculations. RMSE is highly affected by outlier values. Hence, we need to make sure that we remove outliers from our data set prior to using this metric.

6. **AIC (Akaike Information Criteria):** AIC is the measure of fit which penalizes model for the number of model coefficients. Therefore, we always prefer a model with minimum AIC value.

7. **K-Fold Cross Validation: In this method,** we partition the data into k equally sized segments (called 'folds'). One fold is held out for validation while the other k-1 folds are used to train the model and then used to predict the target variable in our testing data. This process is repeated k times, with the performance of each model in predicting the hold-out set being tracked using a performance metric such as accuracy. The most common variation of cross-validation is 10-fold cross-validation. k-fold cross validation is widely used to check whether a model is an overfit or not. For a small k, we have a higher selection bias but low variance in the performances. For a large k, we have a small selection bias but high variance in the performances.

Hosmer-Lemeshow Test: Homer-Lemeshow statistics, which is computed on data after the observations have been segmented into groups based on having comparable predicted probabilities. It scrutinizes whether the observed proportions of events are similar to the predicted probabilities of occurrence in subgroups of the data set using chi square test. Small values with large p-values indicate a good fit to the data while large values with p-values below 0.05 indicate a poor fit.

12.5 BUILDING LOGISTIC REGRESSION

#Step 1: Loading Data into R:

setwd("D:/R data")

loandata=read.csv(file="Housing_loan.csv", header=TRUE)

#Step 2: Data Preparation:

\# Remove the columns ID & Gender from the data

loandata2=subset(loandata, select=-c(ID, Gender))

fix(loandata2)

Step 3: Create Dummy variables:

#The variable "Education" has more than two categories (1: Undergrad,2: Graduate, 3:Advanced/Professional), So we need to create dummy variables for each category to include into the analysis.

#Install & Load the package "dummies" to create dummy variables

install.packages("dummies")

library(dummies)

Edu_dum=dummy(loandata2$Education)

head(Edu_dum)

loandata3=subset(loandata2,select=-c(Education))

loandata4=cbind(loandata3,Edu_dum)

head(loandata4)

#Step 4: Standardization of Data:

Standardize the data using 'Range' method

install.packages("vegan")

library(vegan)

loandata5=decostand(loandata4,"range")

Step 5: Prepare Train & Test data sets:

Take a random sample of 80% of the records for train data.

train = sample(1:1000,800)

train_data = loandata5[train,]

nrow(train_data)

#Take a random sample of 20% of the records for test data

test = (1:1000) [-train]

test_data = loandata5[test,]

nrow(test_data)

#Step 6: Data Summary for the response variable "Loan_sanctioned":

table(loandata5$Loan_sanctioned) #Total Data

table(train_data $Loan_sanctioned) #Train Data

table(test_data$Loan_sanctioned) #Test Data

#Step 7: Build the Logistic regression model

```
model<- glm(Loan_sanctioned~ Age+Experience+
    Income+Family+ Education1+Education2+ Education3,
    data=train_data, family = binomial)
```

Step 8: Check the model Summary and Evaluate the model by obtaining confusion matrix

summary(model)

predict <- predict(model, type = 'response')

table(train_data$Loan_sanctioned, predict > 0.5)

Step 9: Create ROC Curve and Check Area Under Curve

library(ROCR)

pred <- prediction(predict, train_data$Loan_sanctioned)

perf <- performance(pred, 'tpr','fpr')

plot(perf, colorize = TRUE, text.adj = c(-0.2,1.2))

#Step 10: Try with different variable combinations and evaluate the model performance

```
model2<- glm(Loan_sanctioned~ Age+Experience+Income+Family,
    data=loan_train, family = binomial)
summary(model2)
predict <- predict(model2, type = 'response')
#confusion matrix
table(loan_train$Loan_sanctioned, predict > 0.5)
model3<- glm(Loan_sanctioned~ Income+Family,
    data=loan_train, family = binomial)
summary(model3)
predict <- predict(model3, type = 'response')
#confusion matrix
table(loan_train$Loan_sanctioned, predict > 0.5)
```

STEP 13

Decision Trees

13.1 INTRODUCTION

A decision tree is a powerful method for classification and prediction and for facilitating decision-making in sequential decision problems. We can use three types of decision trees i.e., 1. To recommend a course of action based on a sequence of information nodes 2. Classification and Regression trees and 3. Survival Trees. But most of the times we use Decision tree to solve classification problems.

Let us look at some Problems and understand whether it is a Clustering problem or a classification problem.

1. Types of pages on the Web?
2. Whether to approve the personal loan or not?
3. Types of Customers of a shopping mall?
4. Whether this customer will purchase the product or not?
5. What is the next place the tourist would like to visit?
6. Whether the radio signal is supernova, white dwarf or red giant?
7. Types of people in your Facebook/LinkedIn account?
8. Types of e-mails in your inbox?
9. This article is about Sports, Entertainment, politics or science?
10. Types of genes in Human Genome?

What is the difference between clustering and classification?

Whenever you are not given a target to predict, If I say here is the bunch of web pages, I gave only that information, Then we may think about structure of the data, like what types of pages are there, let me do clustering and figure out.

The next question is how many types of customers are there, we are not sure about this. If we are not sure about the target, If we got only the Input data, X, and not Y then we will try to do something like clustering, PCA or any other unsupervised learning technique. But whenever you are given an Input and Output to be predicted, let me say here are the transaction history predict Fraud and not Fraud, Here is an email tell we whether it is spam promotion or main. When I ask you a pointed question, classify it into one of the categories, then it is a classification Problem.

How does it work in the real world? let me take the example of Uber cab, When they started the business, They start getting customer feedback, they do not know what type of feedback they are getting, so, they did clustering. Imagine that they converged on five clusters, once they figured out five clusters they will set up the process for what to do for each cluster. Now these clusters become class labels, Now the next feedback that comes has to map to one of those. If it doesn't then it has to be a separate class. If it belongs to one of the already created groups, then you know what to do, otherwise, you need to create a process around it. So what we need to understand is, whether the structure discovered yet or not.

Imagine the customer complaints go to one email address, then what we need to do is we start to classify them. We can take all 100 thousand complaints, group them into 5-6 types of complaints. How do you map the raw data into types, to discover the types, we need clustering. once we know the types we do classification. we can get new complaints beyond the given types then we create a new class.

Descriptive Vs. Discriminative Classifiers: When people look at the data half of you do one thing and the other half will do the other thing. Some of you may build a model for each class, like what is the structure and shape of the class. this model is called descriptive model that means you describe how the data look like. The other half of you saying hey, how do I discriminate these two. I don't care about the shape of one versus the other I care about the boundary of one versus the other. Discriminative classifiers job is not to worry about the shape of the class, but the boundary. Think like Descriptive classifiers are the home ministry of the country, they care about the shape of the country inside. like these are two countries everybody is interested in their country, But the Discriminative Classifiers are like defense ministry. they are focused more on the boundary. these two are looking at the same data but in different ways.

Let me take my dataset, I have done my feature engineering, Now If I take one class, I just take care of one class, compute the mean and covariance matrix of that class, and the same for the other two then I have these three parameters. When I am computing the mean and covariance of one class I am just considering that class and do not care about the other class. The covariance matrix is going to describe the shape and the mean is going to describe the location.

If I use another kind of classifier, Logistic regression, then it will try to separate the classes. Here both are doing the same thing but in a different way.

13.2 WHAT IS CLASSIFICATION?

In classification, we want to classify the data, in such a way that one group contains points from one class, and another group contains points from other class. we want to divide the space into regions, which should be pure with respect to whatever my class labels are. Let me take an example of India got divided into states, what did they use as criteria. They used Language because they want to come up with sameness so that points in one group is similar to each other and points in other group is similar to each other.

Classification is partitioning the (Feature) space into pure regions assigned to each class. If we have a space like a bunch of points we can move the space, but we can move the partitions around. We have a feature space, which came from all the feature engineering you done, we make sure that they are normalized etc., In that feature space we have a bunch of data points, and we want to create a decision boundary. this boundary will divide the space into smaller regions, now how many decision boundaries I could have chosen? what are the possible ways that I could partition the space? the answer is Infinite. I could have used an infinite number of ways to partition the space into two regions. out of all those infinite ways of a number of partitions I have to find one partition which satisfies the criteria, which maximizes the criteria.

What is that criteria? the criteria is that the each region should be as pure as possible, with respect to the class label. but we are never going to get a perfect partition.

The reasons might be:

- Feature space may not be complete, we may have missed an Important feature.
- Could have outliers,
- Noise in the Features,
- Model may not be perfect,
- Noise in the Label, with all these regions we may not get a perfect model.

That is the reason our job of Data scientist is very challenging. we have a list of reasons why our model is not working. When we classify the space into some regions, and each one has its own set of purity. some classes have more purity when compared to others. Could I have done better? I could have portioned into smaller regions by looking at more features. I could have created nonlinear boundaries, I would have built more complex models to do even better. I could have done so many things to improve this classifier.

Imagine somebody has given this dataset to you to work on, what is the simplest model you can think of? that is the decision boundary of the straight line right, But what is the problem with the simple boundary, it is not as pure as you would like. so the Idea is simplicity does not mean purity or accuracy. What could you do now? If I mathematically write this what type of model is this? Sigma(W0+EWiXi) this is going to give a line, with a line of this level of model complexity you can only do this much. There is going to be only one optimal if I constraint you to a linear model.

Now we say no, Linear is not good enough, we need something more complex, what do we do now? We take Logistic regression and make it more complex by adding nonlinear features. Not just more features, we are limited by features but can we combine the features together. Now I can say something like Sigma(W0+EWiXi + EWijXiXJ) now we get the more complex model, How many parameters do I have now? W0 --> 1,

EWiXi -- > n, EWijXiXJ --> N choose 2 that means when I increase the complexity by adding more parameters we can build more complex decision Boundary.

Imagine a situation where we built a model with a polynomial of degree 2(Second-order we have squares). And another model with a polynomial of degree 9 because there are many almost 9 infections, so it is a 9th-degree polynomial that does a good job, compared to a First-degree polynomial which is a linear classifier.

Can I do even Better? Imagine If I take 100 degrees of the polynomial, There is a very important principle we need to understand here, now think which of these three models is a reasonable model? where would you stop? obviously, nobody want to go to 100-degree polynomial even though it is giving more accurate results.

Let me talk about a general principle which is independent of a problem. Our principle says should I beat the data into submission? if we do the third one we cannot explain the model why did we done that? The major problem is we are over training the training data i.e. we are memorizing the training data we may have lost the ability to generalize since because we have memorized. I might be a good GK quiz master, but I may not think Properly that means I have a good memory but not generalized the model. Typically we choose models neither too simple nor too complex, somewhere in the middle is the correct model, and the art of data science is to find out what is the right level of complexity in the model. I can give you a decision tree or a logistic regression, you can still make a more complex or less complex model, where do you stop is your choice. When you look at the models, the model should do the right thing, it should neither too simple nor too complex. we need to understand the tradeoff. This is what we call as a signal to Noise Ratio. Every data has some structure(Signal) and some Noise. we have to make the model just complex enough to capture the structure but not the noise.

Generalization: The ability to predict or assign a label to a new observation based on the model built from past experience. This is what we call as model complexity and accuracy. What we do normally, we take the data, on the training data if we keep increasing the model complexity, the accuracy increase to the maximum. But that is not our goal. The goal is to look at the Validation or test set which is an Unseen data, at some point, Validation results will start to decrease. This is the point where you should stop increasing the complexity because it is not performing very well on the validation dataset. If we over train something, the model memorizes but it won't learn. So, Over training is something which we need to worry about. We will come back to this, every time when we study a model.

Whenever you are creating a model, we need to understand what were the client expectations. We are interested in creating a generalized model which is accurate. Accuracy is not only the criteria, but we need to look at interpretability of the model. If your model is too complex, it becomes not interpretable, even then it is a problem. Then you may have a highly accurate model, highly generalize model, but not a highly interpretable model. that's another criterion. the other criteria are real time scoring.

If you have a very complex model, that takes one sec to score one data point, Then again you need to cut corners. Therefore we are dealing with all these constraints. I want good generalization, I want interpretability, and high throughput. Now what model do I Build? That is why, it is not obvious what is the right answer. It depends on all these constraints.

If we take two situations here to understand this, Imagine we are building a model for fraud detection, The criteria for the model is accuracy. If I decide to stop the card or let the card go, I do not have a requirement to explain it to someone. Here interpretability is not important, accuracy is Important. Then let me take another situation where we are building a model for credit rating. when I do credit rating, whenever we are rejecting the loan we have to give the top three reasons why we are rejecting the loan, Here interpretability is more important, in a credit rating model. Therefore the models used in credit rating model is very different versus model used in detecting credit card fraud.

We need to ask the following questions whenever we are creating a Model.

◆   What is the Nature of classifier's Decision Boundary?

◆   What is the Complexity of classifier's Decision Boundary?

◆   How do I control the complexity of the classifier?

◆   How do I know when the classifier is complex enough/

◆   How to pick the right classifier to use?

Tree-Based Models: Recursive partitioning is a fundamental tool in data mining. It helps us explore the structure of a set of data, while developing easy to visualize decision rules for predicting a categorical (classification tree) or continuous (regression tree) outcome. Classification and regression trees can be generated through the rpart package.

13.3 STEPS IN CREATING A DECISION TREE.

13.3.1 Grow the Tree

rpart(formula, data=, method=,control=) where,

Formula is in the format outcome ~ predictor1+predictor2+predictor3+ect.

Data =   specifies the data frame

Method = "class" for a classification tree, "anova" for a regression tree

Control = optional parameters for controlling tree growth.

For example, control=rpart.control(minsplit=30, cp=0.001) requires that the minimum number of observations in a node be 30 before attempting a split and that a split must decrease the overall lack of fit by a factor of 0.001 (cost complexity factor) before being attempted.

13.3.2 Examine the results

The following functions help us to examine the results.

printcp(fit) #display cp table

plotcp(fit) #plot cross-validation results

rsq.rpart(fit) #plot approximate R-squared and relative error for different splits (2 plots). labels are only appropriate for the "anova" method.

print(fit) #print results.

summary(fit) #detailed results including surrogate splits

plot(fit) #plot decision tree

text(fit)   #label the decision tree plot

post(fit, file=) #create postscript plot of decision tree

13.3.3 Prune tree

Prune backs the tree to avoid overfitting the data. Typically, you will want to select a tree size that minimizes the cross-validated error, the xerror column printed by printcp( ). Prune the tree to the desired size using prune(fit, cp=). Specifically, use printcp( ) to examine the cross-validated error results, select the complexity parameter associated with the minimum error, and place it into the prune( ) function.

13.4 BUILD THE DECISION TREE MODEL ON HOUSING LOAN DATASET

Let's use the Housing Loan data to predict whether the loan will be sanctioned or not based on Age, Experience, Income, Family size, and Education Level.

Step 1: Install and Load the required Packages

install.packages("rpart")

library(rpart)

library(dummies)

?rpart

Step 2: Loading Data into R:

loandata=read.csv(file="D:\\R data\\Housing_loan.csv", header=TRUE, sep=",")

fix(loandata)

Step 3: remove the columns ID, Gender columns from the data

loandata2=subset(loandata, select=-c(ID, Gender))

fix(loandata2)

Step 4: Create Dummy variables

Edu_dum =dummy(loandata2$Education)

loandata3=subset(loandata2,select=-c(Education))

fix(loandata3)

loandata4=cbind(loandata3,Edu_dum)

fix(loandata4)

Step 5: Standardize the data using 'Range' method

install.packages("vegan")

library(vegan)

loandata_stan=decostand(loandata4,"range")

fix(loandata_stan)

Step 6: Fix the seed to get same data in each time

set.seed(123)

Step 7: Take a random sample of 60% of the records for train data

train = sample(1:1000,600)

loan_train = loandata_stan[train,]

Take a random sample of 40% of the records for test data

    test = (1:1000) [-train]

    loan_test = loandata_stan[test,]

    table(loandata_stan$Loan_sanctioned)

    table(loan_train$Loan_sanctioned)

    table(loan_test$Loan_sanctioned)

#Remove the unnecessary objects

    rm(loandata2, loandata3, loandata4,loandata_stan, Edu_dum, test, train)

Step 8: Build the Decision Tree

fit <- rpart(Loan_sanctioned~ Age +Experience+ Income +Family+

Education1+Education2+Education3, data=loan_train, method="class", control=rpart.control(minsplit=10, cp=0.001))

    #formula is in the format outcome ~ predictor1+predictor2+predictor3+etc.

#data=   Specifies the data frame

#method= "class" for a classification tree, "anova" for a regression tree

#control= Optional parameters for controlling tree growth.

control= rpart.control(minsplit=10, cp=0.001) requires that the minimum number of observations in a node be 10 before attempting #a split and that a split must decrease the overall lack of fit by a factor of 0.001 (cost complexity factor) before being attempted.

Step 9: Display the results

printcp(fit) # display the results

plotcp(fit) # visualize cross-validation results

summary(fit) # detailed summary of splits

Step 10: Plot tree

plot(fit, uniform=TRUE, main="Classification Tree for Housing Loan")

text(fit, use.n=TRUE, all=TRUE, cex=.8)

Step 11: Prune the tree

pfit<- prune(fit, cp= fit$cptable[which.min(fit$cptable[,"xerror"]),"CP"])

#Prune back the tree to avoid over fitting the data. you may want to select a tree size that minimizes the cross-validated error, the xerror column printed by printcp( ).

Conditional inference trees can be created by using party package which provides nonparametric regression trees for nominal, ordinal, numeric, censored, and multivariate responses. You can create a regression or classification tree via the function ctree(formula, data=). The type of tree created will depend on the outcome variable (nominal factor, ordered factor, numeric, etc.). Tree growth is based on statistical stopping rules, so pruning should not be required.

STEP 14

K-Nearest Neighbor Classification

14.1 INTRODUCTION

Prior to discussing KNN, Let us understand the difference between Memory and Learning. Memory is the process of recording, storing and retrieving information. In Memory, we keep the data and always go back to it whenever it is necessary. Learning is the process or behavior of acquiring knowledge. It is not simply the acquiring and storage of information, but the ability to implement the information and make use of it in practical circumstances. If we build a model which is a much more compressed version of the data, then we forget about the data, we use the only model in future. that is how our brain works. So, We can say learning is a process that will modify a subsequent behavior. Memory, on the other hand, is the ability to remember past experiences.

K-Nearest neighbor is a simple algorithm that stores all available cases and classifies new cases by a majority vote of its k neighbors. This algorithm segregates unlabeled data points into well-defined groups. KNN classifier is one of the most simple and beautiful classifiers. Imagine a scatter plot with data points of pink and Blue classes, In which, Pink data points are more prominent at top left corner, and at the right bottom Blue is more prominent, but there is a lot of noise in the data. that's how the real data is. Now, if I give you a new data point and ask you to classify that. What will you do? you start to find the nearest point to the given new data point based on the distance, Assume the nearest is pink. what do You will do? You will assign this new data point to pink. This is called 1 Nearest Neighbor.

It's something like this, You want to watch a movie, you called one of your friends, and asked was it good or bad. Whatever he says, you will do. Is that what you will do? no, then what will you do? We call more people, go online and read reviews, You watch the trailer and then you decide, right. So the decision process depends on external inputs, the more input you get, The more robust your decision will be. Instead of using 1 Nearest neighbor, what can I do? I can use 2 nearest neighbors, Now I called 2 friends, First guy said, go watch it and another says don't watch it. Now I am even more confused. So, in K nearest neighbors we avoid using K as an even number. If I go with

3 nearest neighbors it once again changes based on the number of points majority. If I go further up again the Label may change. and so on and so forth.

How do you control complexity here? What is the simple model and complex model in K nearest Neighbors? They take the raw data which is Pink and Blue, Assuming it's a test example, They used a particular K value, and said if I use the three nearest neighbors, What would be my label? Pink or blue?. This is the space and we partitioned it into 2 Regions. Nobody says the regions has to be nice and beautiful. Now the blue region has some purity and any point belongs to the blue will be assigned to Blue region.

Now, what happens when K increases. Regions have changed for some of the points, as the K increase, we get smoother boundaries and our model becomes more and more robust to noise. Earlier it as responding to noise too much. What is the learning here? Higher the K, more robust the model is and less complex the model is. The model looks almost like linear regression. We need to consider few questions while building a classifier. What are the parameters? did we learned any parameters?

In Logistic regression did we learned any parameters? Weights are my parameters. Things that I learned. In K-means Clustering the cluster centers are the parameters, and K is the Hyperparameter. In K nearest Neighbors K is called a hyperparameter. It is something that you give to the system to control the complexity. In the case of KNN, there are no parameters. There is no Model. Therefore in KNN the training time is Zero because it is not learning anything. That is why it is called as a non-parametric model.

What is the downside of this KNN?. How long do you need to score a data point? Imagine if I give you 100 thousand data points in the training set, and said here is a new data point comes in, what is that you need to do? You need to measure the distance from all the 100 thousand points, and then sort it and pick the top K, see what are their labels, that exercise is order N, in the training time. Would you use such a classifier, for real-time decisions?. While picking a Modeling technique, we look at not just the accuracy of it, but look at the computation time even. If I need to build a model that need to trained very quickly, My data is changing very fast, then you need a model which does not have training time at all. The key here is how do you define your distance function. defining distance function is the toughest task. Imagine two variables like age and Income how do you define the distance between these two?

The distance between two LinkedIn profiles, Distance between two gene sequences etc., two sound signals, two documents on the web, two tweets, two movies and goes on. Let me take a simple example of cancer gene sequence, we have around 10 thousand cancer patients gene sequences and 1 million gene sequences of non-cancer patients. when a new data point comes in, what we need to decide is we need to check with all the billion gene sequences match it to all the gene sequences, and compute distances between them, find K and so on, this is pretty hard to do. So, While choosing the modeling technique, we need to think about, What is K?, What is distance Function?, Will I be able to score Faster now? all these things.

The another problem with KNN is, the actual distance it would not take into account. I am just saying Top K. I am not saying How Far. so, this is one more problem with KNN since it loses the distance information. One more problem with KNN is it not robust to noise. Unless you increase the K too much, it is not very noise robust.

14.2 HOW TO SELECT APPROPRIATE K VALUE?

Choosing the number of nearest neighbors i.e. determining the value of k plays a significant role in determining the efficacy of the model. Thus, selection of k will determine how well the data can be utilized to generalize the results of the kNN algorithm. A large k value has benefits which include reducing the variance due to the noisy data, the side effect being developing a bias due to which the learner tends to ignore the smaller patterns which may have useful insights.

kNN Algorithm – Pros and Cons

Pros: The algorithm is highly unbiased in nature and makes no prior assumption of the underlying data. Being simple and effective in nature, it is easy to implement and has gained good popularity.

Cons: Indeed kNN algorithm doesn't create a model since there's no abstraction process involved. Yes, the training process is really fast as the data is stored verbatim but the prediction time is pretty high with useful insights missing at times. Therefore, building this algorithm requires time to be invested in data preparation to obtain a robust model.

14.3 BUILD KNN MODEL ON DIABETIC DATASET

Detecting Diabetes: Machine learning finds extensive usage in pharmaceutical industry especially in the detection of Diabetes and Cancer. Let's see the process of building this model using kNN algorithm in R Programming.

Step 1: Data collection:

We will use a data set of diabetic patients to implement the KNN algorithm and thereby interpreting results. The data set consists of 500 observations and 7 variables which are as follows: In real life, there are dozens of important parameters needed to measure the probability of Diabetes but for simplicity purposes let's deal with 7 of them.

- Pat_Id
- Gender
- OGTT
- DBP
- BMI
- Age
- Diabetic

Step 2: Data Exploration

setwd("D:/R data") # Let us import the 'Diab.csv' data file. This command is used to point to the folder containing the required file.

Diabdata <- read.csv("Diab.csv", header = TRUE,stringsAsFactors = FALSE) #This command imports the required data set and saves it to the Diabdata data frame.

stringsAsFactors = FALSE #This command helps to convert every character vector to a factor wherever it makes sense.

str(Diabdata) #We use this command to see whether the data is structured or not. We find that the data is structured with 7 variables and 500 observations. If we observe the data set, the first variable 'Pat_Id' is unique in nature and can be removed as it does not provide useful information.

Step 3: Data Preparation

#Remove the first variable(Pat_Id) from the data set.

Diabdata <- Diabdata[-1]

The data set contains patients who have been diagnosed with either Diabetic or NonDiabetic

#A quick look at the Diabetic attribute through tells you that the division.

table(Diabdata$Diabetic)

The variable Diabetic is our target variable i.e. this variable will determine the results of the diagnosis based on the other numeric variables. #If you want to check the percentage division of the Diabetic attribute, you can ask for a table of proportions:

*round(prop.table(table(Diabdata$Diab)) * 100, digits = 1)*

#Profound Understanding Of Your Data

summary(Diabdata)

#You can also refine your summary overview by adding specific attributes

summary(Diabdata[c("OGTT", "BMI")])

Step 4: Normalization:

This feature is of paramount importance since the scale used for the values for each variable might be different. The best practice is to normalize the data and transform all the values to a common scale.

#We can perform feature normalization, by first making your own normalize function:

normalize <- function(x) {

num <- x - min(x)

denom <- max(x) - min(x)

return (num/denom)

}

Diab_norm <- as.data.frame(lapply(Diabdata[3:6], normalize))

summary(Diab_norm)

fix(Diab_norm)

Let's check using the variable 'BMI' whether the data has been normalized.

summary(Diab_norm$BMI)

Step 5: Creating training and test data set:

The kNN algorithm is applied to the training data set and the results are verified on the test data set. For this, we would divide the data set into 2 portions in the ratio of 60: 40 for the training and test data set respectively. You may use a different ratio altogether depending on the business requirement.

#Training And Test Sets

set.seed(1234)

Indicator <- sample(2, nrow(Diab_norm), replace=TRUE, prob=c(0.6, 0.4))

#We can then use the sample that is stored in the variable Indicator to define your training and test sets:

Diab.training <- Diab_norm[Indicator==1, 1:4]

Diab.test <- Diab_norm[Indicator ==2, 1:4]

Our target variable is 'Diabetic' which we have not included in our training and test data sets.

Diab.trainLabels <- Diabdata[Indicator ==1, 7]

Diab.testLabels <- Diabdata[Indicator ==2, 7]

Step 6: Training a model on data:

The knn () function needs to be used to train a model for which we need to install a package 'class'. The knn() function identifies the k-nearest neighbors using Euclidean distance where k is a user-specified number.

install.packages("class")

library(class)

Now we are ready to use the knn() function to classify test data. Let us Build our Classifier, To build your classifier, we need to take the knn() function and simply add some arguments to it.

Diab_pred <- knn(train = Diab.training, test = Diab.test, cl = Diab.trainLabels, k=11)

Diab_pred

The value for k is generally chosen as the square root of the number of observations. knn() returns a factor value of predicted labels for each of the examples in the test data set which is then assigned to the data frame Diab_pred. The result of this command is the factor vector with the predicted classes for each row of the test data.

Step 7: Evaluation of Your Model:

To check models performance, We can import the package gmodels:

install.packages("gmodels")

#If you have already installed this package, you can simply enter

library(gmodels)

#Then we create a cross tabulation or a contingency table.

CrossTable(x = Diab.testLabels, y = Diab_pred, prop.chisq=FALSE)

There were no cases of False Negatives (FN) meaning no cases were recorded which actually are Diabetic in nature but got predicted as NonDiabetic. The FN's if any poses a potential threat for the same reason and the main focus to increase the accuracy of the model is to reduce FN's.

The total accuracy of the model is 60 %((TN+TP)/35) which shows that there may be chances to improve the model performance

Step 8: Improve the performance of the model

This can be taken into account by repeating the steps 3 and 4 and by changing the k-value. Generally, it is the square root of the observations and in this case, we took k=10 which is a perfect square root of 100.The k-value may be fluctuated in and around the value of 10 to check the increased accuracy of the model. Do try it out with values of your choice to increase the accuracy. We need to remember that to keep the value of FN's as low as possible.

STEP 15

Bayesian Classifiers

15.1 INTRODUCTION

Bayes theorem is a mathematical theorem applying by which we are trying to find out the relationship between the data and the class. We need to think if this is the data then what should be the class. Here we are trying to do the mapping between data and class.

1. What is the probability that the customer will respond given this offer and coupon.
2. What is the probability that you have cancer or not cancer given that specific gene sequence?

Let me discuss Bayes rule. Let us understand why is it such an important thing.

$$P\left(\text{Class}|\text{Data}\right) = \frac{P\left(\text{Class}\right)P\left(\text{Data}|\text{Class}\right)}{P\left(\text{Data}\right)}$$

P(Class) $\rightarrow$ Class Prior

P(Data|Class) $\rightarrow$ Data Likelihood given Class

P(Data) $\rightarrow$ Data Prior(Marginal)

P(Class|Data) $\rightarrow$ Posterior Probability(Probability of class after seeing the data)

Let me talk about the very simple property of joint probability distribution, If I say, P(a,b) I can write it in two types, as P(a) times p(b given a) or P(b) times p(b given a). Let us understand this with an example, Imagine you are a doctor, you are waiting for the next patient to come in. do you already know what the disease will be? Can you guess what the disease would be? whatever we know without looking at the data, we call that as prior. When I asked to interview a candidate in a software organization, without looking at the candidate, without looking at his resume what can I say whether the candidate will be hired or not? How will I do that? I look at all the people, who attended interviews and what fraction of them hired. this is called prior probability.

The same doctor has seen many patients in the past and diagnosed them correctly, then we have an expectation on the data point to classify them into that class (data Likelihood gave class). Then I need to consider even that what is the probability of such a patient will ever come to me.(Data Prior Marginal). Based on this information, I need to predict the future. Given this new data point, tell me what is the probability of this class. That's what we are trying to do, So, Bayes theorem in not a mathematical jugglery of conditional probability, It is really a way to connect your past experience with your future prediction. There are a whole bunch of modeling techniques just based on Bayes theorem. Most of the machine learning spends time on Data Likelihood gave class. Maximum Likelihood means what is the likelihood of, this data coming from this class, and we just try to do a max on it. There are two ways to think about Bayesian theorem. 1. Maximum Likelihood Decision 2. Maximum A posterior probability decision.

15.2 THINKING LIKE A BAYESIAN

This is just applying our probability theory in decision making. I am going to give you a scenario, we are going to convert that English sentences as probabilities and conditional probabilities and we will go through computing the posterior probabilities. Imagine that you are the manufacturer of the machine, Take hundred people whom you know that have cancer and test them, if the statement says the machine will give Correct positive result 95% of the times.

P (Test_positive | Has_Cancer) =.95, P (Test_Negative | Has_Cancer) =.05

That means even the machine is saying negative and you have cancer, it does not mean you do not have cancer. What are data and Class here? The test result is the data, Cancer no cancer is the output.

Imagine that you are the manufacturer of the machine, Take hundred people whom you know that do not has cancer and test them. If machine gives Correct negative result 90% of the times.

P (Test_Negative | No_Cancer) =.9, P (Test_Positive | No_Cancer) =.1

And, only 0.8% of the entire population has cancer:

P(Has_Cancer) =0.008, P (No_Cancer) = 0.992

Here we are dealing with two variables: 1. whether the patient has cancer or not, 2. Test Came out Positive or Negative.

Now Let me ask What is the prior probability that test is positive? To Answer this we need to calculate two things 1. patient has cancer is the machine showing positive or not., 2. patient does not have cancer is the machine showing positive or not.

= [P (Test_positive | Has_Cancer) * P(Has_Cancer) +

P (Test_Positive | No_Cancer) * P (No_Cancer)]

=0.95*0.008 + .1*0.992 = 0.1068

What is the prior probability that the test is negative?

= [P (Test_Negative | Has_Cancer) * P(Has_Cancer) +

P (Test_Negative | No_Cancer) * P (No_Cancer)]

=0.05*0.008 + .9*0.992 = 0.8932

This is how we think like a Bayesian. I can't measure how many times it is going to be positive. It depends on what kinds of patients are tested on. We cannot just observe the data by ignoring the class label.

Let me take an example, I would like to predict will you sneeze today? It depends on what are the causes of sneezing and whether you are going to expose those causes then we can say whether you sneeze or not.

Now let me ask the other question. If a new patient walks in and the test is positive, we apply the Bayes theorem. What is the probability of cancer if the test is positive?

P (Has_Cancer | Test_Positive)

= [P (Test_positive | Has_cancer) * P (Has_Cancer) / P (Test_Positive)]

= [(0.95 * 0.008) / 0.1068] = 0.07116

What is probability of cancer if test is negative?

P (Has_Cancer | Test_Negative)

= [P (Test_Negative | Has_cancer) * P (Has_Cancer) / P (Test_Negattive)]

= [(0.05 * 0.008) / 0.8932] = 0.00045

even the evidence says that the patient has cancer but we need not to worry because the prior is very low. For calculating NaiveBayes we need to know how to calculate Mean and covariance and Bayes probability calculation.

Mahalanobis distance: When you take the data, Take the PCA of the data, what do you do when you take PCA of the data you essentially remove the covariance in it and then you compute the distance, so that becomes Mahalanobis Distance.

Bayesian Classifier Decision Boundary: Remember that we discussed 2 types of classifiers in the previous chapters, 1. The shape of the class 2. decision Boundary. In Bayesian Classifier Decision Boundary we use both. what we are doing is we are creating one Gaussian per each class and where ever the two are equal that is our decision boundary.

15.3 NAIVE BAYES

NaiveBayes is a very important class of Bayesian classifiers.

Conditional Independence: we know Independence between two variables, If I say two events are happening and they are completely random, what can we say about the joint probability? P(A, B)= P(A)* P(B).

Just let us assume that we walked into a doctors chamber and we said we have fever and body ache. do you think these two symptoms are independent? No, there is a common cause for both of the above symptoms. doctors try to figure out the common cause of all the independent symptoms. Let us say a viral infection causing these two symptoms. So, The viral Infection is the cause. Then We can write this statement like this: P (Fever, Body ache | Viral) = P (Fever | Viral) * P (Body ache | Viral) this is what is called Conditional independence.

Again going back to the Bayes theorem, I want to find out the probability of Viral Infection given that the patient has Fever and Body ache.

P (Viral | Fever, Body ache) = [P (Fever,Body ache | Viral) * P (Viral)] / P(Fever, Body ache).

15.4 BUILD NAIVE BAYES FROM THE DIABETIC DATASET

Step 1: Get Your Data:

#load in the data set with the following command:

setwd("D:/R data")

Diabds <- read.csv("Diab.csv", header = TRUE)

fix(Diabds)

Step 2: Know Your Data:

It is a better idea to inspect the data set by executing

head(Diabds)

str(Diabds)

names(Diabds)

summary(Diabds)

Step 3: Prepare your Data:

Remove the first variable(Pat_Id) from the data set.

Diabdata <- Diabds[-1]

Step 4: Load the required Packages:

Install and Load the e1071 package

install.packages('e1071',dependencies=TRUE)

library(e1071)

Step 5: Split the dataset

Diab_test = sample(1:nrow(Diabdata),200)

Diab_train = setdiff(1:nrow(Diabdata),Diab_test)

Step 6: Build The Model

Diab_nb = naiveBayes(Diabdata[Diab_train,2:5],Diabdata[Diab_train,6])

Dia_res = predict(Diab_nb,Diabdata[Diab_test,2:5])

Step 7: Display a confusion matrix

table(Dia_res,Diabdata[Diab_test,6])

Step 8: Compute accuracy

cm_Diab = table(Dia_res,Diabdata[Diab_test,6])

#compute the sum of diagonal values in a matrix

correct = sum(diag(cm_Diab))

accuracy = correct / sum(cm_Diab)

STEP 16

Neural Networks

16.1 INTRODUCTION

Neural Network (NN) has neurons and layers in its architecture. 3 layers in Neural Network are **Input Layer, Hidden Layer,** and **Output Layer**. Each of these layers has units or neurons in it.

Human Neural Network: The basic computational unit in the nervous system is the nerve cell or neuron. A neuron has 1. Dendrites (inputs) 2. Cell body 3.Axon (output). A neuron receives input from other neurons, Inputs gets summed up and, Once input exceeds a critical level, the neuron discharges an electrical pulse that travels through the body, down the axon, to the next neuron. This spiking event is also called depolarization and is followed by a refractory period, during which the neuron is unable to fire. The axon endings almost touch the dendrites or cell body of the next neuron. Transmission of an electrical signal from one neuron to the next is effected by neurotransmitters, chemicals which are released from the first neuron and which bind to receptors in the second. This link is called a synapse. The extent to which the signal from one neuron is passed on to the next depends on many factors, e.g. the amount of neurotransmitter available, the arrangement of receptors, amount of neurotransmitter reabsorbed, etc.

Let us understand EM algorithm, In K-means clustering what we were done is we assigned the clusters to data points and compute the mean, once we compute the mean we reassign the data points. Because we don't know the model, we start somewhere and move ahead from there.

Applications of neural network:

1. Robotics – Navigation, Vision Recognition
2. Medicine – Storing medical records
3. Speech Recognition
4. Stock market prediction
5. Data compression
6. Image processing
7. Face recognition
8. Cab or truck position tracking

9.   Signal Processing

10.   Recognizing Handwritten characters.

16.2 WHY NEURAL NETWORKS?

The neural network is a breakthrough algorithm in machine learning. First, let us understand why is logistic regression not enough? When there are more than 2 classes, we so far have suggested doing the following: Assign one output node to each class, Set the target value of each node to be 1 if it is the correct class and 0 otherwise, Use a linear network with a mean squared error function. There are problems with this method. First, there is a disconnect between the definition of the error function and the determination of the class. A minimum error does not necessary produce the network with the largest number of correct prediction.

New Interpretation: The output of yi is interpreted as the probability that i is the correct class. This means that the output of each node must be between 0 and 1. The sum of the outputs of all nodes must be equal to 1.

Let us take XOR problem, The EXCLUSIVE-OR gate is a two-input, one-output gate, this is a classic example why we need a neural network. XOR. Just take the two-way switch mechanism in our home if both we on or both were off the switch is considered to be off. If either one is on the switch is considered to be on. It says if both are zeros or both are ones we get value X and either one is zero/One we get value Y. XOR gates produce a 0 when both inputs match. When searching for a specific bit pattern or PRN sequence in a very long data sequence, a series of XOR gates can be used to compare a string of bits from the data sequence against the target sequence in parallel. The number of 0 outputs can then be counted to determine how well the data sequence matches the target sequence.

How many lines do we need to draw to differentiate the data points like this? Minimum two since with one I cannot completely differentiate the data. Here we need to understand that Logistic regression in not enough because the data complexity is more than the model complexity.

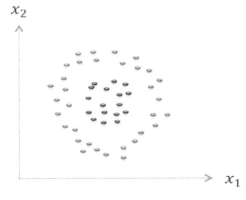

Now what kind of lines can I Have? do I have a unique solution?

We can get different solutions. there are actually four different solutions for this. one of that is given in the image, at least with these two lines, I can do something. whatever we do, ultimately what I am doing is I am partitioning the space into multiple pure regions.

However I do it, whether I do it by fixing a Gaussian, or a mixture of Gaussians, with two Gaussians per class, Imagine If I would have to solve the same problem with descriptive classifier what I would have done, is one Gaussian enough per class? No, one Gaussian is not enough. In both cases whether you go descriptive or discriminative, it is independent, the nature of the data says, one Gaussian is not enough and one line is not enough. so, therefore, I need two Gaussians or two lines in the discriminative classifier.

When we say there are multiple local minimums, what do we mean is the bottom line is one local minima, that means it will give me a good answer, if you look at the other one, that is another set of parameters which will also, give me highly pure regions, that is another local minima. So, we can understand that there are multiple solutions for this problem. That is what makes this kind of algorithms challenging.

Let me take one equation per line, Now I have two lines, is it enough? the first line only says whether you are on this side or that side. It does not say what is the class. The above line also says whether you are on this side or that side. It does not even say what is the class. We need somebody to listen to both the lines and combines the output, and then say what is the final class. That is what a neural network looks like. This is the simplest neural network, this is one neuron equal to one line, this is the another neuron which is another line, and look at the weights, this line says 2 times X1 plus 2 times X2 minus 1 that gives you one line. the other line can be explained in the same way. The above point like the manager of the team, listens to everybody and takes their output, and weighs them accordingly and pushes them forward. This is the final decision he is taking. Remember we discussed Hierarchies, like each engineer doing one thing, and we need somebody to combine their output and deliver the final decision.

By now we understood why we needed Neural network. Let us learn how to interpret them. The neural network is nothing but more than one logistic regression and a combiner on top of them. This is also called a multilayer Perceptron. Let us think in this way like if the new data point is above the first line and below the second line, then we say it is Red. otherwise, you are Blue. Generally when we make rules and decisions it is a bunch of And Statements. Let's take it once again, like if you are on this side of the line and this side of the other line then what is the Answer?. Let us look at the line that means you are above the bottom line. And below the top line, if both these conditions are true then you are red. In a rule-based system, these are given to you, you do not learn them, and we just make a rule out of those statements. But in Neural networks we are creating a rule in this fashion. in decision tree also the whole path is a rule. Let me connect this to healthcare situation that if you have a Chills and Fever the problem might be Malarial Fever.

Neural networks are also called as multilayered Perceptron. If I have a raw data in which one group of points are embedded in another group of points, Now tell me how many lines do I need? Now I need at least three or more. What are we saying? every hidden unit is a line. the way the interpretation goes is every time we add a unit, it's one line another hidden unit is another line and so on. depending on the complexity of the problem, I can add more and more hidden units and it can give me more and more lines. and then we add a constant.

Remember what we said earlier about a neuron, the nature of neuron does not change, it's input can change. The neuron in the middle is taking info from the left two units and the threshold is there on top. Activation and a switch make up a neuron. the right most neuron does not take the raw input. it is a generalized linear model, it takes middle points as inputs. It does not know anything about the raw data, that means roles of each neuron is very clear, they know what it is supposed to do and what it is not.

Our basic computational element (model neuron) is often called a node or unit. It receives input from some other units, or perhaps from an external source. Each input has an associated weight w, which can be modified so as to model synaptic learning. The unit computes some function f of the weighted sum of its inputs:

$$y_i = f\left(\sum_j w_{ij} y_j\right)$$

- The weighted sum $\sum_j w_{ij} y_j$ is called the **net input** to unit i, often written *neti*.
- Note that wij refers to the weight from unit j to unit i (not the other way around).
- The function f is the unit's **activation function**. In the simplest case, f is the identity function, and the unit's output is just its net input. This is called a **linear unit**.

If I give you a neural network architecture, Let's Say I have D inputs, and always we have a constant X0 is always 1. There is always a constant term per layer. and we have H hidden units, and C classes at the end,

Let us understand in the case of Diabetic Data where the input and output are fixed. We cannot do anything about it. What can we change the number hidden units and number of hidden layers? That gives you the complexity. If complexity goes on to a specific level the accuracy increases.

Now tell me how many weights are there that I am learning. for one hidden unit, I have W0 and number of Inputs that means D+1 weights. Then how many hidden units I have. H hidden units. that is the number of parameters just from here to here, for the hidden unit in the next layer, it is computed once again, in the same way, for the end class, it is computed like (H+1)C. so final answer is (D+1) H + (H+1)C. this way we can compute the parameters for any complexity. Let me put it in simple words once again, a Neural network is fully connected, think of the first neuron, it is connected to all the D inputs, each input has a weight, think of this as g(W0+W1X1 +... WdXd) this is the logistic regression. this gives me the output of one neuron.

How many parameters are there? what are the degrees of freedom? How many parameters it is learning?. It is learning (D+1) and it is true for other units even, since all of them are learning D+1 weights, so (D+1)H. Now the same logic is applied to the next layer, and so on. Let us take the C output units, here the inputs will be the hidden units of the previous layer (H+1) and I have C such units. so C(H+1). This way we can compute a number of parameters for any complexity.

Let's say we have 10000 pixels in your retina, that is your input, tell me how many different slants of lines you can tell me. and imagine a watch how many tilts we can detect visually, it is 60. we can even do fine grade but let us say 60. that means from 10000 inputs you came to 60 hidden units. Now if I say, not only straight lines, what about curves, you can detect all kinds of curves, you can detect curves with different orientation, I can go on and on and I can have more than the number of inputs, similarly in the next layer, if I say circles, oval, triangles, and others, if we going up in the hierarchy it does not mean you are reducing the number of features. it's a combinatorial explosion actually. With a small number of things, the degree of combinations goes up and up actually. This is what a deep network does actually. it handles so much of complexity.

That's what nature says, it's nature is so complex, if an animal or a human has to understand this much of complexity, We need a very complex neural network, but it cannot create neurons which are different, so it said How can I create a complex network, with the building block which is same and what it has to do, is change the building blocks. That's the beauty of a neural network. Every neuron is still doing the same thing. all it is doing is a linear combination of its inputs, followed by a logistic function. all the billion neurons are doing exactly the same thing. with that much of simplicity, you get this much of complexity. because the architecture is different.

You may ask me what about gradient kind of classification. It's a kind of logistic regression it has a gradient. Let us imagine initially these lines are very random if we see how this look before training, it is very chaotic. we won't even know which of this line becomes this specific line. we need a mechanism to do soft transitions of lines. Now Imagine a team of new hires, we through them 5 problems, and said I need somebody to detect the vertical lines, somebody to detect the horizontal line, and they all do some sort of struggle to do what. So, finally, some guy says let me find out this line and you go and find out another line, without all of us doing the right thing we cannot do the classification. That behavior emerges from initially random kids to a genius.

16.3 HOW DO YOU DECIDE THE NUMBER OF HIDDEN LAYERS AND UNITS?

It is the matter of importance, how do you decide the number of clusters in K-means clustering, How do you decide the depth of a decision tree, How do you decide the K in K-nearest Neighbors, How do you decide the width of the parzan window, these are all hyperparameters. These control the complexity of the model. that is something you have to give.

We do not decide the number of Inputs and we do not decide the number of outputs, and we do not even decide the weights. we learn the weights. The more complex the model is higher could be the accuracy, but you need to give the optimum complexity.

People asks me like what is the right model to use? that is not the right question, the right question is do you care about the interpretation of the output or do you not? Let me take two situations in the first situation they want to detect fraud, and they do not care that it has to be explained it to the consumer, why we are calling it a fraud. here the interpretation of the model is not important, the accuracy of the model was important. In this case, we use the neural network because it is very hard to interpret it.

If you care about Interpretation we need to use decision tree, Let me take another example, in another case if you reject the loan for somebody, you need to give the reasons, you can't just reject the loan, you have to have valid reasons, therefore here interpretation of the model is very important, you cannot build a neural network here, even at the cost of less accuracy we use decision trees since interpretability is high. So while deciding between decision trees and neural networks, you need to ask which is more important for you is its accuracy or interpretability.

There are other such criteria, the criteria are how fast your model is changing?. If you are dealing with a very dynamic environment, one model which you built for summer is not going to work for winter, then you need to rebuilt your model, so the criteria are can I rebuild the model quickly? How long does it take to build the model?

Another criterion is, is your decision real time or Batch? If the decision is the real time you have to build a model which can quickly process the data and take the decision. taking a decision on credit card fraud has to be real time decision. But if you are building a credit rating model, you can use a decision tree. Then you may ask me one more doubt, can I use KNN? It might be very accurate, but it will take a huge amount of time, because in KNN it computes the distance from all the points, so it cannot be used in real time. So, the right question is not which model is good? The right question is which criteria do you care about?

let me tell you what are the four criteria you need to look at.

1. Decision-making real-time or not?
2. Accuracy you need high or not?
3. how quickly your model has to be rebuilt?
4. Interpretability does it matter or not?

think of this four questions and then you decide which modeling technique you need to use.

The Idea of complexity is like this, Imagine what happens if they put one more hidden layer on top of this existing layer. If you want more complexity the another direction to go is Increase the number of layers.

Let us understand the equation, The output from the previous layer the jth unit from the previous layer, giving you weighted sum, doing a logistic on top of it, gives you the output of the next layer. this is the recursive equation, because of the g in layer n, leads to the g in n+1. It's keep going on and on in the forward direction, this is what a neuron does but where it sits makes the difference.

We talked about generalized linear models, We said that if we want to do a linear regression, you do not want to do it only on X, You can do it on any function of X, That's what a hidden unit does as opposed to the input unit, and then, this is still a linear model, I am starting J from 0, because W0 is also part of this linear equation, I do not want to say W0 plus something so therefore, We put a 1 here and start with W0 directly. Then we can say, this is a linear model, we can't deal with linear we need to make sure our neurons are limited because imagine, if your neuron can really fire very high, your brain will burst, so we kept a logistic function, then the higher end becomes flattered, so, logistic function on a linear combination, leads to the output of a neuron.

We can denote the Neural network algorithm like the following:

$$z_k^{(\ell+1)} = f\left(\sum_{j=0}^{S_\ell} z_j^{(\ell)} w_{jk}^{(\ell)} \right)$$

where:

$Z_k^{(l+1)} \rightarrow$ Activation of *kth* Neuron in the Next Layer

$f \rightarrow$ Activation Function

$Z_j^l \rightarrow$ Activation of jth Neuron in the Current Layer

$W_{jk}^l \rightarrow$ Weights(Parameters)

Let me recapitulate the same thing, there are different components, you could map this to the structure of the neuron, so the inputs are these guys, the dendrites coming from the previous layer, they are all aggregated, they sent through Axon, to the other side, after the activation function, this is the output of the neuron which goes to the future neurons. The neuron doesn't know what to do with the output, it just says if you connect to me, this is what you are going to get. Activation functions job is to make sure that the linear thing, doesn't go infinitely, in positive or negative direction, so it just curtails that in a systematic way, there are different kinds of activation functions.

Just look at the shapes of them, they are all doing the same thing, whatever is the input that is coming, the input can be very large, I want to contain that range of output into 0 to 1. for that reason we need something to bind the output. That's why we inserted the logistic regression in the first place. so the shape changes. All these functions are doing the same thing with slight variation, the concept is near the boundary, you need to be able to do something smooth, so it doesn't look like hard Perceptron, and away from the boundary you have to be able to contain the values between 0 to 1. if those two properties are there, then we can define all kinds of such activation functions, this is all coming from neuroscience, they do a lot of experiments to figure out, what is the right function. One problem with the neural networks was, I know how to train the weight of this layer, the more internal the layer is, the harder it is to correct because it depends on so many things that eventually happened, which led to right or wrong.

Think of this in this way, if I ask the kid to recognize A versus 4, the neurons that detect lines play a role, the neuron that detects character A play a role, that neuron will get the direct input, the child said A and it is not A. so, he has to fix himself, but that fixation will go further back, and say did you detect the line properly. could that be the reason that you could not detect A properly? This is how the backpropagation works. This was the big invention in neural networks, which makes neural networks even to train the internal nodes. if it is one layer it is easy. What we do, when we wake up in the day, we take the data we put it forward, and we get the feedback, we take the feedback, and back propagate and learn, and so on.

Let us look at the same thing on Housing _loan data, in Housing _loan data how many inputs we have, it is 4, and we have a constant, then I build a model, and I have 3 outputs, I do not know how many hidden units I really need, it could be less or more than the class, we play around and train the neural network for Housing_loan dataset. Later I take one example in this row, it has some features, the neurons already have some weights, based on the weights it is going to give me some activation here, which is going to tell me whether I am this side or that side of the line, and we have three classes, Imagine that I decided that the new point is class 3. How does the output look like, I expect 1 at that place of the class and 0 in other two classes. this is how you convert a classification problem to a neural network problem.

Since the neuron is not perfect yet, it may give you 0.9, 0.4, 0.6 for three classes, because it is not fully trained yet, then we find the error and we need to backpropagate the error, therefore it is called error back propagation. here, in this case, I need to back propagate the -0.9 of error because we always say target minus the actual (0–0.9) is the error. so the weights causing the error so high now they will go down. in the second case, even the weights will go down but not as much as the first situation. and in the third case, we get 0.4 so we increase the weights so that the activation is higher now. So the error has to be propagated from the top down and the output has to go from the bottom up.

Let us take the example of Google uses to detect pictures they may have 100's of layers. It becomes far more complex to interpret, but it does something very powerful. Whenever you are using neural networks, first learn enough about the data, decide how complex it is, by that way we get a good starting point, and assume that three looks like good enough, then you try with 2 and 4 even, and see if it improves. if it improves on 4 let me try with 5 even and so on. It's a matter of hit and trial.

That is the reason the data scientist job is bit challenging, he can go back to raw analysis, build a very raw model, then look back and learn and create the model again and so on. The real big breakthrough was how do you learn this weight? The amount of load going to this way is proportional to the involvement of that unit in the decision. The idea is higher your weight the more blame you have to take.

Let me take business scenario, How much error this director made is proportional to few things like How much was the total error and what was he committed with this unit and how much is the error other made and what was his involvement in that decision, together is the amount of correction this unit needs to do? The back propagation first accumulates the error and sends the same to my predecessors. I do the same thing to my juniors because based on their commitment I committed to my V.P. It is like this, forward pass is accumulating info and distributing and backward propagation in accumulating error and distributing. Look at the beauty of neural networks, same neurons doing exactly the same thing, but the way they are connected they keep passing on the info and error and keep learning. so the weights keep learning.

This was the breakthrough and because of this we all have credit cards today. Imagine if we did not apply Neural networks to fraud detection problem, banks would have been closed the credit card system. The neural network is stateless, it basically takes one input and gives you one output, and it takes that error and back propagates. It does not know anything about the next example. Remember IID,(Independent and Identically Distributed), neurons are stateless, it does backward and forward.

In a lot of other situations you need state, for example, you want to decide how loudly you want to speak to your friend, it depends on where you are. here the state is in which room you are in and how far or near he is to you. Basically, think the state in an environment where the previous state also contributes to the next output. In that situation where the plain neural networks do not work, they invented some new thing called recurrent neural networks. In this what it does? it takes the current input, it generates a state, but then it remembers the state that becomes once again the input, now we say here is your current input, here is your state, together we will decide what should be the next output.

Whenever you have sequential learning problems like you are learning to predict a stock market, you need to remember the previous state, and if you want to predict the next word in the sequence of words, you need to remember the state. whenever you have a state thing going on there is an internal feedback loop that goes back. because this is the memory part in the learning. like our brain has a notion of memory. there would be a decaying thing involved here because I cannot give the same weight to yesterday's learning and one month back learning. it's like an exponential decay. think about this, you know what you did today morning but you do not know what you did 5 days ago. so your state is always current.

Another type of neural network is compression network, If we take a picture with the camera, I will get a picture in png format it is very large, then what do I do, I compress it. when you compress that is not good enough you should be able to uncompressing. only then you get jpeg image. Here in this situation, it is not learning anything called supervised, it is not saying X to Y what it is saying is, X to a compressed version of X, and then it uncompressed, now the input and the output are supposed to be the same. if the compression is good, what they do they take the same numbers, put the same numbers in the output, and then they learn the network, this is an unsupervised learning technique because there is no Y variable. You can use this where ever you use PCA, PCA is the linear projection Compressed neural networks are the non-linear projections. This is like speech encoder, our phones use this, your voice first gets compressed, then gets transmitted on the channel, then the another guy receives it, he has the same encoder-decoder, he uses his decoder to uncompressing it, and what you hear is a slight variation of what the original one.

Here we are not learning the mapping between something to something else. like we are mapping the features to class labels. but this one is a compression problem that means, you have to learn a compression and decompression so that the overall effect overall reconstructing error should be minimized.

Learning rate is another parameter we have to specify like we specified the Hidden units. generally, we start with small learning rate and if we feel it is very slow then we increase the learning rate, But at some point, if we increase the learning rate too much, it gets overtrained, so we need to find the optimal learning rate. An important consideration is the learning rate μ, which determines by how much we change the weights w at each step. If μ is too small, the algorithm will take a long time to converge. Conversely, if μ is too large, we may end up bouncing around the error surface out of control, the algorithm diverges.

16.4 BUILDING NEURAL NETWORKS ON HOUSING_LOAN DATASET

Step 1: Install and Load the required packages

install.packages('neuralnet')

library("neuralnet")

library(dummies)

library(vegan)

Step 2: Loading Data into R:

loandata=read.csv(file="D:\\R data\\Housing_loan.csv", header=TRUE, sep=",")

fix(loandata)

Step 3: Remove the columns ID column from the data

loandata2=subset(loandata, select=-c(ID))

```
fix(loandata2)
Edu_dum =dummy(loandata2$Education)
loandata3=subset(loandata2,select=-c(Education))
fix(loandata3)
loandata4=cbind(loandata3,Edu_dum)
fix(loandata4)
```

Step 4: Standardize the data using 'Range' method

```
loandata_stan=decostand(loandata4,"range")
fix(loandata_stan)
# Set the seed to get same data in each time
set.seed(123)
```

Step 5: Take a random sample of 60% of the records for train data

```
train = sample(1:1000,600)
loan_train = loandata_stan[train,]
# Take a random sample of 40% of the records for test data
test = (1:1000) [-train]
loan_test = loandata_stan[test,]
table(loandata_stan$Loan_sanctioned)
table(loan_train$Loan_sanctioned)
table(loan_test$Loan_sanctioned)
rm(loandata2, loandata3, loandata4,loandata_stan, Edu_dum, test, train)
```

Step 6: Build the Neural Net

```
nn <- neuralnet(Loan_sanctioned~ Age+Experience+
    Income+Family+ Education1+Education2+ Education3,
    data=loan_train, hidden=c(2,3))
out <- cbind(nn$covariate, nn$net.result[[1]])
fix(out)
dimnames(out)  =  list(NULL,c  ("Age","Experience","Income","Family","Education1","
Education2", "Education3","nn-output"))
```

Step 7: View top records in the data set

head(out)

plot(nn)

Step 8: Data preparation for classification matrix

p=as.data.frame(nn$net.result)

colnames(p)="pred"

pred_class <- factor(ifelse(p$pred > 0.5, 1, 0))

a <- table(pred_class, loan_train$Loan_sanctioned)

*recall <- a[2,2]/(a[2,1]+a[2,2])*100*

Step 9: Retrieving required columns from the data

test_data2=subset(loan_test, select=-c(Loan_sanctioned))

new.output <- compute(nn,covariate=test_data2)

p=as.data.frame(new.output$net.result)

colnames(p)="pred"

pred_class <- factor(ifelse(p$pred > 0.5, 1, 0))

a <- table(pred_class,loan_test$Loan_sanctioned)

*recall <- a[2,2]/(a[2,1]+a[2,2])*100*

recall

Step 10: Play with different node structures (3), (2,2), (4,3)

We can take different hidden layers and different hidden inputs and create model check their accuracy and recall percentages. Then finalize the model based on accuracy and recall on Validation (Testing) dataset.

STEP 17

Support Vector Machines

17.1 INTRODUCTION

Support Vector Machine (SVM) is a classification and regression prediction tool that uses machine learning theory to maximize predictive accuracy while automatically avoiding over-fit to the data. Whenever we think about creating a model, we think about few things like complexity, determinism, sampling, features etc.

Complexity: In a good modeling technique, we should be able to control its complexity, in the case of a mixture of Gaussians complexity is the number of components, with Neural network complexity, are the number of hidden units and hidden layers.

Determinism: I want the algorithm to produce the same thing again and again with the same training data. Imagine the other algorithms depending on the starting point it goes somewhere else. that is not a desirable property, but that is what happens when you have a complex model. Perceptron, neural networks, K-means Clustering has the same problem, It does not produce the same result every time.

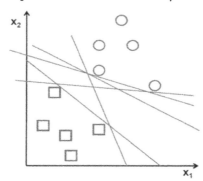

Optimal Hyper Plane: The classification problem can be constrained to the contemplation of the two class problem without loss of generality. In this problem, the goal is to distinct the two classes by a function which is induced from presented examples. The goal is to produce a classifier that will work well on unseen examples, i.e. it generalizes well. Here there are many potential linear classifiers that can separate the data, but there is only one that maximizes the margin (maximizes the distance between it and the nearest data point of each class). This linear classifier is termed the optimal separating hyperplane.

Let us say I have a dataset with two class problem, I want to build a classifier, and I use Perceptron as a classifier. Perceptron no matter where it starts, it keeps on learning and as soon as it stops making mistake, it stops learning. We can have many perceptrons (Infinite) for a dataset which has two class problem. All these perceptrons have the same cost of misclassification which is Zero. so all these can be valid models. But what is wrong with them? first thing is They are not deterministic, that means every time when I start somewhere else, it gives me a different result. There is one more problem, there are some points which are really close to the boundary. so it is a fragile model. If I get a slightly different data point, It might make a big mistake. That's not what we want. we wanted the model to be more robust. Now since we have these problems we should try for something better than the existing models that're How SVM came into the picture. Now think intuitively, where the decision boundary should be. It should be far away from both the data points, that means in the middle of the closest data points. the decision boundary has to be robust. small changes and noise should not affect the decision boundary.

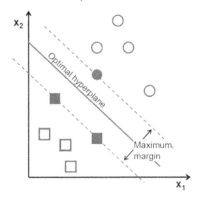

Imagine these are two villages, and you want to make a road in between them, Road has to be as wide as possible, But there is a constraint if I want to build a wide road, but I do not want to break the houses. What we are trying here is we try to build a boundary as robust as possible, without breaking houses on the either side. What would be the good classifier?. I want a linear classifier such that I want to draw a line on either side and stop where the first house is. and then look at the width of this road. this is also called a maximum margin classifier.

Here not all the data points are Important, the data points which are near the boundary are Important. The question is can you find the houses along which I can make the road. Let us see how a mathematician solves a machine learning problem. If I have a hyperplane and I want to measure the perpendicular distance between the origin and line it is going to be this much (-B/|w|).

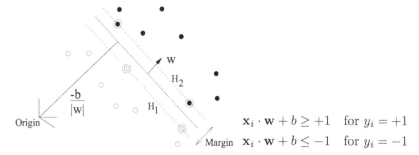

$$\mathbf{x}_i \cdot \mathbf{w} + b \geq +1 \quad \text{for } y_i = +1$$
$$\mathbf{x}_i \cdot \mathbf{w} + b \leq -1 \quad \text{for } y_i = -1$$

So I want to find the W and B, what we are trying here is if we could find the middle of the road, if you go +1 here, or -1 here there should be nothing (No Houses) in between. So the equation looks something like this, Xi (The nearest data point), for all the house that are on one side of the road, this condition should hold (W+B >= +1) for all the houses that are on the other side of the road, the other condition should hold. (W+B <= -1).

Now remember what the Perceptron do, Perceptron says that Xi W + W0 is >0 or <0. In Perceptron as soon as you cross the boundary you are on the other side. there is no notion of margin. It's just a line. In SVM what we are doing is we need a margin of errors, so Instead of saying 0 we will put 1 and -1 here. That is the only difference between a Perceptron which has Zero Margin Versus SVM which has Maximum margin, that means we are increasing the thickness of a Perceptron. If we put both the above equations in a single one we get Yi(Xi.W+B)-1 >=0. In supervised learning, we always define the objective function and solve it. An objective function has two parts. (Maximize, Constraints). Here we are trying to maximize the margin under the constraint that No damage to the Houses.

Now tell me how many constraints here? Let us go back to linear programming situation, In Linear programming, we draw a bunch of lines, which are considered as linear constraints. Therefore we think that should be at one side of the line. I cannot draw a line as wide as possible because I have a constraint that I cannot break the houses. I have N (Total Number of Data Points) Constraints now since I cannot break any of the house.

In the initial diagram, All the lines are possible but we need to further fine tune my objective function to get the unique line or optimal solution. The line which is furthest from both the sides is the best since it maximizes the margin. When we Formulate the problem, it only means that if this was the line, What would be the margin be, what would be the constraints be, and then we solve for what would be the line. It's like Let X be the solution, and solve for X.

If we look at the mathematics, Geometry says If I drew a perpendicular line from origin to any line, then the length is (-b/w). then when we look at other two lines one is above and the other is below, their length would be (1-b/w) and (-1-b/w), Margin would be one equation minus other equation. B gets canceled and what we get is 2/W.

Objective: $\dfrac{1}{2}\|w\|^2$

Constraint: $y_i\left(x_i \cdot w + b\right) - 1 \geq 0 \quad \forall i$

Here we have objective function and a set of constraints. The constraints are the number of data points since we cannot break any of the house I the village each data point(House) is my constraint.

Our goal is to optimize the objective function with the given constraints. In this situation, Lagrange proposed a Multiplier which says we need to pay some penalty for violating each constraint. Suppose if you violate the ith constraint you pay Alpha I Ci(x) penalty. That alpha is called the Lagrange Multiplier. Then we sum over all the penalties.

In Support vector machine algorithm we can apply three tricks:

1. Primal to Dual conversion
2. Slack Variables
3. Choosing the Kernel

Just think this our objective function is to maximize the margin so violating the constraint should minimize the value. So, we need to subtract the overall summation of the penalties from the Objective function which we are trying to maximize. So finally the equation should look like:

17.2 PRIMAL TO DUAL CONVERSION

Lagrange Multiplier: Let me take a simple example so that you can understand this whole theory. Let us Imagine your wife called you and said by 7.30P.M she planned to go out for shopping. Now your goal is to reach home early. This is your objective function. You have a set of constraints like finish your work early, don't drive very fast, don't jump the signal, don't hit any vehicle etc., if you violate any of this constraint you will be penalized the penalty differs from one constraint to another. So finally we sum over all the penalties and subtract that from the objective function which you are trying to maximize. What we need to think is did we violated any constraint or not while reaching our objective. If we did not violate any constraint our penalty would be zero.

$$L_p \equiv \frac{1}{2}\|w\|^2 - \sum_{i=1}^{l} \alpha_i y_i \left(x_i \cdot w + b\right) + \sum_{i=1}^{l} \alpha_i$$

The Lagrange primal problem looks like the above and what we need to understand is we want to convert this primal problem into a dual problem so that I can get rid of w and b.

Because if I know alpha I can compute w and b. it is like this, If I know what are those houses which I should not break while laying the road, I can plan my road accordingly. The dual form of the equation looks like this in which we do not have w and b.

$$L_D = \sum_i \alpha_i - \frac{1}{2} \sum_{i,j} \alpha_i \alpha_j y_i y_j x_i \cdot x_j$$

The important thing to remember is We can maximize the margin by identifying those data points (houses) which will form the boundary, essentially these are called support vectors. These are vectors because these are the points in a high dimensional space and these are the points(vectors) supporting the plane(Decision Boundary).

We have one constraint for one data point and after we solve this, it generated a bunch of alpha values for each data point. These alpha values are saying that these point is near the decision boundary or not. The important thing to understand here is most of the alpha values are zero because most of the data points are inside the boundary(most of the houses are inside the village). What we need to understand here is the higher the value of alpha the higher that point is on the road.

17.3 SLACK VARIABLES

Till now we are discussing the data which is linearly separable. Now think about what happens if the data points are not linearly separable. Just Imagine the real world data which is usually not linearly separable. Here we need to apply one more trick called Slack Variables. If the training set is not linearly separable, we use the standard approach to allow the fat decision margin to make a few mistakes for some data points like outliers or noisy examples which are inside or on the wrong side of the margin. We then pay a cost for each misclassified example, which depends on how far it is from meeting the margin requirement. To implement this, we introduce slack variables. A non-zero value for ξ_i allows x_i to not meet the margin requirement at a cost proportional to the value of ξ_i.

The optimization problem is then trading off how fat it can make the margin versus how many points have to be moved around to allow this margin. The margin can be less than 1 for a point x_i by setting $\xi_i > 0$ but then one pays a penalty of $C\xi_i$ in the minimization for having done that. The sum of the ξ_i gives an upper bound on the number of training errors. Soft-margin SVMs minimize training error traded off against margin. The parameter C is a regularization term, which provides a way to control overfitting: as C becomes large, it is unattractive to not respect the data at the cost of reducing the geometric margin; when it is small, it is easy to account for some data points with the use of slack variables and to have a fat margin placed so it models the bulk of the data.

Observe the above data points and given constraints. There is a possible road with these data points, but

$$x_i \cdot w + b \geq +1 - \xi_i \ \text{ for } \ y_i = +1$$
$$x_i \cdot w + b \leq -1 + \xi_i \ \text{ for } \ y_i = -1$$
$$\xi_i \geq 0 \forall i.$$

What kind of model is this?

- What is the model?
- What are the parameters?
- What is complexity?

17.4 KERNEL TRICK

If the data is nonlinearly separable, that means if the data cannot be separated with the straight line then we want the SVM to project the data to higher dimensional space to make it possible linearly or perform the linear separation. This is called kernel Trick.

17.5 BUILDING SUPPORT VECTOR MACHINE ON HOUSING_LOAN DATASET

setwd("D:/R data")

#Loading Data into R:

loandata=read.csv(file="Housing_loan.csv", header=TRUE)

#Data Preparation: Remove the columns ID from the data

loandata2=subset(loandata, select=-c(ID))

fix(loandata2)

 #The variable "Education" has more than two categories, (1: Undergrad, 2: Graduate, 3:Advanced/Professional), #so we need to create dummy variables for each category to include into the analysis.create dummy variables for the categorical variable

#"Education" and add those dummy variables to the original data.

install.packages("dummies")

library(dummies)

#Install & Load the package "dummies" to create dummy variables

Edu_dum=dummy(loandata2$Education)

head(Edu_dum)

loandata3=subset(loandata2,select=-c(Education))

loandata4=cbind(loandata3,Edu_dum)

head(loandata4)

#Standardization of Data: Standardize the data using 'Range' method

install.packages("vegan")

library(vegan)

loandata5=decostand(loandata4,"range")

#Prepare train & test data sets, Take a random sample of 60% of the records for train data

train = sample(1:1000,600)

train_data = loandata5[train,]

nrow(train_data)

#Take a random sample of 40% of the records for test data

test = (1:1000) [-train]

test_data = loandata5[test,]

nrow(test_data)

#Data Summary for the response variable "Loan_sanctioned":

table(loandata5$Loan_sanctioned)

#Train Data

table(train_data $Loan_sanctioned)

#Test Data

table(test_data$Loan_sanctioned)

#Classification using SVM:

install.packages("e1071")

library(e1071)

#Install & Load the package e1071 to perform SVM analysis.

x = subset(train_data, select = -Loan_sanctioned)

y = as.factor(train_data$Loan_sanctioned)

?svm

model = svm(x,y, method = "C-classification", kernel = "linear", cost = 10, gamma = 0.1)

#Kernel: The kernel used in training and predicting. You might consider changing some of the following parameters, depending on the kernel type.

Cost: cost of constraints violation (default: 1)-it is the 'C'-constant of the regularization term in the Lagrange formulation.

Gamma: parameter needed for all kernels except linear.

summary(model)

Test with train data

pred = predict(model, x)

table(pred, y)

Test with test data

a = subset(test_data, select = -Loan_sanctioned)

b = as.factor(test_data$Loan_sanctioned)

pred= predict(model, a)

table(pred, b)

model2 = svm(x,y, method = "C-classification", kernel = "radial", cost = 10, gamma = 0.1)

summary(model2)

#Test with train data

pred = predict(model, x)

table(pred, y)

#Test with test data

pred = predict(model, a)

table(pred, b)

STEP 18

Ensemble Learning

18.1 INTRODUCTION

Let us move into another dimension of modeling techniques, called ensemble methods. Till now we discussed individual models, and we see how to handle increasing complexity but let us think what to do if these models are not good enough? If linear SVM is not enough we go to polynomial SVM of degree2 and then degree 3, if these are not enough we go to nonlinear SVM with RBF kernel, there is a way to keep increasing the complexity but as we seen increasing the complexity will increase accuracy up to one specific level only. In this method, we keep increasing the complexity.

The another big area of improving the model performance is to engineer better features. You may say that I extracted a bunch of features, and built a model, I built the best possible model with this set of features, I can't do better than that, let me go back to my data, let me improve my features, add few more features, again build the complex model and this cycle goes on. with raw features, we may need complex models, but with better feature engineering we may need a simple model. Let us take another approach to improving our model performance, called ensemble learning. In this, instead of learning on the complex model, we learn many simple models and combine them. That is the approach to increase the overall model complexity.

The ensemble is nothing but a group of things as a single collection. So far what we are doing is, we are taking some input, we extract some features, we train the model, we increase the complexity of the model, and obtaining the output. An ensemble is a technique for combining many weak learners in an attempt to produce a strong learner. In statistics and machine learning, ensemble methods use multiple models to obtain better predictive performance than could be obtained from any of the principal models. The term ensemble is usually reserved for methods that generate multiple hypotheses using the same base learner. Evaluating the prediction of an ensemble typically requires more computation than evaluating the prediction of a single model, so ensembles may be thought of as a way to compensate for poor learning algorithms by performing a lot of extra computation. Fast algorithms such as decision trees are commonly used with ensembles.

18.2 BAGGING

Bagging is a technique used to reduce the variance of our predictions by conjoining the result of several classifiers modeled on diverse sub-samples (Data Sampling) of the same data set.

Create Multiple Data Sets: Sampling is done with replacement on the original data and new datasets are formed. The new data sets can have a fraction of the columns as well as rows, which are generally hyper-parameters in a bagging model. This helps in making robust models, less prone to overfitting. We Build Multiple Classifiers on each data set, and predictions are made.

Combined Classifiers: The predictions of all the classifiers are combined using a mean or mode value depending on the Business problem. The combined values are mostly more robust than a single model. A Higher number of models are always better performance than lower numbers. It can be hypothetically shown that the variance of the combined predictions is reduced to 1/n (n: number of classifiers) of the original variance.

Steps in **B**ootstrap **aggregating (Bagging)**:

- We start with a sample size N
- We create a large number of samples of the same size. The new samples are generated from the Training dataset using sampling with replacement Method. So they are not identical with the original sample.
- We repeat this many times maybe 1000 times, and for each of these bootstrap samples, we compute its mean, which is called bootstrap estimates.
- Create a Histogram with these estimates, if provides an estimate of the shape of the distribution of the mean from which we can find out, how much the mean fluctuates.

The key principle of the bootstrap is to provide a way to simulate repeated observations from an unknown population using the obtained sample as a basis. We draw $n^*<n$ samples from D with replacement (means same sample can be in multiple draws). We apply a classifier C1 and repeat it with a different sample and a new classifier C2. The '**m**' models are fitted using the above m bootstrap samples and combined by averaging the output for regression or voting for classification.

18.3 RANDOM FORESTS

Random Forest is an Ensemble learning method for classification and regression, by constructing multiple decision trees. Random Forests are reasonably fast and easy to use. They can handle sparse data and with Random Forest we can overcome the overfitting problem. Random Forest can take a different subset (sample) of data with replacement and it can even sample the features, that means it performs Data Sampling(Observations) as well as Feature sampling(Variables). Finally, the decision is taken by majority voting.

In a decision tree, one decision tree is built and in a random forest algorithm, many decision trees are built during the process. A vote from each of the decision trees is considered in deciding the final class of a case or an object, this is called ensemble process. Since many decision trees are built and used in a process of Random Forest algorithm, it is called a **Forest**. We know that A data frame has two dimensions 1. Rows and 2. Columns. For a building, a decision tree, samples of a data frame are selected with replacement along with selecting a subset of Columns for each of the decision trees. Both sampling of the data frame (**Data Sampling**) and selection of a subset of the variables(**Feature Sampling**) are done randomly.so we call this as **Random Forest.** Random forests improve predictive accuracy by generating a large number of bootstrapped trees based on random samples of variables, classifying a case using each tree in this new "forest", and deciding a final predicted outcome by combining the results across all of the trees.

18.4 BUILDING A MODEL USING RANDOM FOREST

Step 1: Install and Load Required Packages and Library

install.packages('randomForest')

library(randomForest)

Step 2: Read the data and create a data frame.

Diab<-read.csv(file="D:/R data/Diab.csv",header = T)

Step 3: Explore data frame

fix(Diab)

str(Diab)

Step 4: Set the seed to make reproducible results

set.seed(4848)

Step 5: Create Train and Test Datasets Train(70%), Test(30%).

#Take a random sample of 70% of the records for Train data

train = sample(1:500,350)

train_data = Diab[train,]

nrow(train_data)

#Take a random sample of 30% of the records for test data

test = (1:500) [-train]

test_data = Diab[test,]

nrow(test_data)

Step 6: Build the Model by using Random Forest Algorithm

fit <- randomForest(as.factor(Diabetic) ~ Gender + Age + OGTT + DBP + BMI,

　　data=train_data, importance=TRUE, ntree=400)

Step 7: Check what variables were important:

varImpPlot(fit)

Step 8: Validate your Model by Predicting the unseen data

Prediction <- predict(fit, test_data)

Final <- data.frame(Id = test_data$Pat_Id, Diabetic = Prediction)

fix(Final)

Step 9: If you are not happy with the model results, you can try conditional inference trees, which make their decisions using a statistical test rather than a purity measure.

install.packages('party')

library(party)

fit <- cforest(as.factor(Diabetic) ~ Gender + Age + OGTT + DBP + BMI,

　　data=train_data, controls=cforest_unbiased(ntree=700, mtry=3))

Prediction <- predict(fit, test_data, OOB=TRUE, type = "response")

In random forest we force the model to predict our classification by temporarily changing our target variable to a factor with only two levels using as.factor(). The **importance**=TRUE argument allows us to inspect variable importance, and the **ntree** argument specifies how many trees we want to grow. If you were working with a larger dataset you try with lesser number of trees, or restrict the complexity of each tree using **nodesize** as well as reduce the number of rows sampled with **sampsize**. You can also override the default number of variables to choose from with **mtry**, but the default is the square root of the total number generally works fine. We can use **replace** Takes True and False and indicates whether to take sample with/without replacement **proximity** Whether to calculate proximity measures between rows of a data frame options.

The Out of Bag(OOB) Error Estimate: In Random forests, there is no need for cross-validation or a separate test set to get an unbiased estimate of the test set error. Each tree is constructed using a different bootstrap sample from the data. About 1/3 of the cases are left out of the bootstrap sample and not used in the construction of the Kth tree. Put each case left out in the construction of the kth tree down the kth tree to get a classification. In this way, a test set classification is obtained for each case in about 1/3 of the trees. At the end of the run, take j to be the class that got most of the votes every time case n was oob. The proportion of times that j is not equal to the true class of n averaged over all cases is the oob error estimate, this has proven to be unbiased in many tests.

Shortcomings in Random forest Variable Importance: Random Forest is very popular as a variable selection technique. However, it has some drawbacks as well. If independent variables are of different type random forest variable importance measure can be misleading. If independent variables are all categorical but having different categories, random forest variable importance measure can be misleading. To overcome both the above problems, we should use conditional inference forest i.e. cforest. If independent variables are correlated, random forest variable importance measure can be misleading. Even, the conditional forest does not remove Multicollinearity problem completely. It solves collinearity problem to some extent.

18.5 BOOSTING

Boosting is a more systematic way of improving performance through combining various classifiers. Consider creating three component classifiers for a two-category problem through boosting.

1. Randomly select n1 < n samples from D without replacement to obtain D1 and train weak learner C1.
2. Select n2 < n samples from D with half of the samples misclassified by C1 to obtain D2 and train weak learner C2.
3. Select all remaining samples from D that C1 and C2 disagree on and train weak learner C3. Final classifier is vote of weak learners.
4. If the bootstrap replicated approximations were correct, then bagging would reduce variance without changing bias. In practice, bagging can reduce both bias and variance. For high-bias classifiers, it can reduce bias and for high-variance classifiers, it can reduce variance.

Adaboost: In Adaboost, instead of drawing samples every time, a weight is assigned to each sample. The weight is the probability of the sample to get selected in a classifier. It works with binary classifiers that are better than random coin tosses (error less than 0.5). The idea is to adjust the weight such that those records that are incorrectly classified to be selected for the second level of classification by the second classifier. So, if a classifier makes an error in predicting the variable, the variable's weight increases. Then the classifier is defined as a linear combination of all the weak classifiers. The result is the mode of prediction of all the classifiers.

Let us say, we have a data set (x1,y1),...(xm,ym) where x is the value and y is whether it was picked by a classifier. So, y takes either -1 or 1. We start with initial weights, We choose the classifier such that the error with respect to the distribution is minimal and less than 0.5. A weak classifier has less than 50% error but still is unsatisfactory (50% is a coin toss case and hence more than 50% error is not allowed even for a weak classifier).

$$\alpha_t = \frac{1}{2}\log\frac{1-\epsilon_t}{\epsilon_t} \geq 0.$$

Here, It is the error of an individual classifier. After we classify with the first weak classifier, we update the weights such that

$$D_{t+1}(i) = \frac{D_t(i)}{Z_t} * \begin{cases} e^{-\alpha_t} & if\ h_t(x_i) = y_i \\ e^{\alpha_t} & if\ h_t(x_i) \neq y_i \end{cases}$$

$$= \frac{D_t(i)e^{-\alpha_t y_t h_t(x_i)}}{Z_t}$$

Z_t is a normalization factor to ensure that D is always a distribution. So, if a particular field is correctly classified, the exponential term is low (as y is positive). Hence, weight is low. For those that are misclassified, y is negative and hence exponential is large and hence weights go up. We continue with all the weak classifiers and at every stage, we choose the classifier that minimizes the error. In this way, this is a greedy algorithm.

In the early iterations, boosting is primary a bias-reducing method and in later iterations, it appears to be primarily a variance-reducing method. The training error is defined at any round is the fraction of misclassified observations.

$$\frac{\sum_{i=1}^{m}\left(H(x_i) \neq y_i\right)}{m}$$

The training error drops exponentially fast. Choose αt that minimize Zt. It has no parameters to tune (except for the number of rounds). It is fast, simple and easy to program. It comes with a set of theoretical guarantee (e.g., training error, test error) Instead of trying to design a learning algorithm that is accurate over the entire space, we can focus on finding base learning algorithms that only need to be better than random. It can identify outliers: i.e. examples that are either mislabeled or that are inherently ambiguous and hard to categorize. However, the actual performance of boosting depends on the data and the base learner. Boosting seems to be especially susceptible to noise.

Bagging versus Boosting: Bagging always uses resampling rather than reweighting. Bagging does not modify the distribution over examples or mislabels, but instead always uses the uniform distribution. In forming the final hypothesis, bagging gives equal weight to each of the weak hypotheses.

18.6 BUILDING A MODEL USING ADABOOST

Step 1: Loading Data into R:

setwd("D:/R data")

loandata=read.csv(file="Housing_loan.csv", header=TRUE)

Step 2: Data Preparation:

Remove the columns ID & Gender from the data

loandata2=subset(loandata, select=-c(ID, Gender))

fix(loandata2)

Step 3: Create dummy variables for the categorical variable "Education" and add those dummy variables to the original data.

#Install & Load the package "dummies" to create dummy variables

install.packages("dummies")

library(dummies)

Edu_dum=dummy(loandata2$Education)

head(Edu_dum)

loandata3=subset(loandata2,select=-c(Education))

loandata4=cbind(loandata3,Edu_dum)

fix(loandata4)

Step 4: Standardization of Data:

Standardize the data using 'Range' method

install.packages("vegan")

library(vegan)

loandata5=decostand(loandata4,"range")

Step 5: Prepare train & test data sets

#Take a random sample of 60% of the records for train data

train = sample(1:1000,600)

train_data = loandata5[train,]

nrow(train_data)

#Take a random sample of 40% of the records for test data

```
test = (1:1000) [-train]
test_data = loandata5[test,]
nrow(test_data)
```

Step 6: Data Summary for the response variable "Loan_sanctioned":

```
#Total Data
table(loandata5$Loan_sanctioned)
#Train Data
table(train_data $Loan_sanctioned)
#Test Data
table(test_data$Loan_sanctioned)
```

Step 7: Classification using Adaboost:

```
#Install & Load the package — ada to perform SVM analysis.
install.packages("ada")
library(ada)
x = subset(train_data, select = -Loan_sanctioned)
y = as.factor(train_data$Loan_sanctioned)
Ada_20=ada(x,y,iter=20,nu=1,loss="logistic", type="discrete")
summary(Ada_20)
```

Step 8: Add testing data set

```
a = subset(test_data, select = -Loan_sanctioned)
b = as.factor(test_data$Loan_sanctioned)
Ada_t20=addtest(Ada_20,a,b)
pred = predict(Ada_t20, a)
table(pred, b)
```

Step 9: Plot Ada_t20

```
plot(Ada_t20,TRUE,TRUE)
```

Step 10: Try with 50 Iterations

```
Ada_50=ada(x,y,iter=50,nu=1,loss="logistic", type="discrete")
summary(Ada_50)
```

Ada_t50=addtest(Ada_50,a,b)

pred = predict(Ada_t50, a)

table(pred, b)

#Plot Ada_50

plot(Ada_t50,TRUE,TRUE)

#Step 11: Try with different Iterations like iter=100,500,1000 to check the accuracy and fix a model.frame()

Index